No one else

can match the effectiveness, the simplicity, or the appeal of the

SPECTRUM READING SERIES

Students gain meaningful practice—independently

With the SPECTRUM READING SERIES students not only get the practice they need in essential reading skills, they also enjoy being able to do it on their own.

In grades one through six, each lesson features an illustrated story followed by exercises in comprehension and basic reading skills. Because the same format is used consistently throughout, your students will have little trouble doing the lessons independently. And each two-page lesson can be finished easily in one class period.

Students develop and refine key reading skills.

- **Comprehension** exercises help students go beyond understanding of facts and details to drawing conclusions, predicting outcomes, identifying cause and effect, and developing other higher level comprehension skills.
- **Vocabulary development** builds on words from the reading selections. In addition to learning synonyms, antonyms, and words with multiple meanings, students develop sight vocabulary and learn to use context as a clue for meaning.
- **Decoding** exercises refine students' abilities to "attack" and understand new reading words.
- **Study skills** are developed by helping students apply their reading skills to new tasks, such as using reference materials, reading graphs, and applying other everyday life skills.

Reading selections captivate and motivate.

Students get their best reading practice by actually reading. That's why the selections in the SPECTRUM READING SERIES, in addition to offering practice in skills, also motivate students to read—just for fun.

Students quickly become friends with the characters in these entertaining stories. And they enjoy new levels of reading success—thanks in part to carefully controlled vocabulary and readability as well as beautiful illustrations.

The program adapts completely to any teaching situation.

The SPECTRUM READING SERIES can be used in many different ways.

- For the whole class . . . for intensive reinforcement of reading skills or to supplement a basal reading program.
- For reading groups . . . to provide skills practice at the appropriate levels.
- For individual use . . . to help build a completely individualized program.
- For at-home practice . . . to expand on skills learned in the classroom.

Index of Skills for *Reading Grade 5*

Numerals indicate the exercise pages on which these skills appear.

Knowing the Words

Abbreviations—19, 27, 29, 37, 65, 71
Antonyms—9, 11, 27, 37, 55, 69
Classification—3, 5, 13, 25, 35, 39, 53, 57, 63
Homophones—15, 23, 41, 49, 53, 77
Idiomatic and figurative language—7, 13, 23, 25, 39, 47, 63, 67, 79, 83
Multiple meanings—11, 15, 17, 25, 33, 43, 51, 75
Sight vocabulary—*All lessons*
Synonyms—13, 21, 31, 45, 49, 57, 73, 81
Word meaning from context—*All activity pages*

Working with Words

Compound words—3, 21, 33, 43, 49, 65, 77
Possessives—3, 7, 13, 17, 27, 29, 31, 35, 37, 45, 53, 61, 71, 75, 81
Prefixes and suffixes—5, 9, 11, 15, 17, 19, 23, 25, 39, 41, 47, 51, 55, 57, 59, 63, 67, 69, 73, 79, 83, 85

Reading and Thinking

Author's purpose—17, 21, 27, 37, 41, 51, 55, 71, 81
Cause and effect—7, 11, 19, 21, 23, 25, 37, 39, 47, 49, 57, 59, 63, 73, 75, 77, 85
Character analysis—3, 9, 13, 29, 31, 47, 57, 81
Comparison and contrast—17, 33, 35, 39, 45, 55, 65, 83, 85
Context clues—5, 7, 9, 23, 25, 35, 37, 39, 43, 45, 49, 53, 59, 67, 69, 77
Drawing conclusions—5, 9, 13, 15, 17, 27, 29, 33, 43, 51, 63, 67, 71, 73, 75, 77, 79, 83, 85
Facts and details—3, 9, 11, 19, 23, 25, 33, 35, 37, 43, 49, 51, 53, 55, 61, 63, 65, 67, 69, 71, 75, 77, 79
Fact and opinion—3, 11, 27, 29, 31, 41, 51, 53, 61, 65, 81
Main idea—5, 9, 11, 15, 17, 19, 21, 27, 31, 33, 35, 39, 47, 59, 61, 63, 67, 69, 75, 83
Mood and tone—5, 7, 13, 15, 23, 35, 85
Predicting outcomes—3, 11, 15, 21, 23, 29, 33, 43, 47, 49, 59, 77, 85
Sequence—7, 13, 19, 25, 31, 41, 45, 57, 73, 79
Summarizing—15, 27, 55, 61, 71, 73

Learning to Study

Dictionary use— 3, 9, 11, 23, 31, 33, 35, 45, 49, 53, 67, 83
Following directions—*All activity pages*
Charts, graphs, and maps—5, 43, 55, 59, 61, 71, 77, 85
Life-skills materials—13, 15, 21, 37, 47, 65, 79, 81
Outlines—17, 19, 25, 29, 51, 63, 73, 79, 81, 85
Reference materials—3, 7, 27, 29, 39, 41, 57, 69, 75

SPECTRUM READING
Grade 5

Table of Contents

It Was All a Dream

Read this story to discover Tom's dreams.

1 "This is a great interview, Tom. The story is surely front-page material," beamed Uncle Max. "You're turning into *The Kendall Bulletin's* star reporter."

2 "I owe it all to you, Uncle Max. Ever since I was a kid, I've wanted to put my writing talent to use by becoming a journalist like you," said Tom.

3 "Well, you knew a good thing when you saw it," joked Uncle Max, patting Tom's shoulder.

4 "You always believed I'd make it, didn't you? You taught me that the only limits I have are those I set for myself," replied Tom thoughtfully. "Between you and Mom, how could I miss? Hey, what's that commotion? Is there a fire somewhere, or is it another story breaking? What's going on?"

5 "Wake up, wake up, Tom. Your alarm clock is noisy enough to wake up everybody in the neighborhood. Get up, or you'll miss your bus."

6 "Mom, is that you?" Tom mumbled.

7 "Who else do you suppose would be trying to rouse you at this hour of the morning?" answered Mrs. Ellis.

8 "Wow, what a fantastic dream I was having! I was a reporter just like Uncle Max, and I was investigating a bank robbery for *The Kendall Bulletin.*"

9 "Someday, Son, your dreams may come true. But in the meantime, don't you think you'd better get yourself out of this bed and ready for school where you're already a star reporter?" coaxed Mrs. Ellis.

10 "Oh, Mom, how can you compare what Uncle Max does at the *Bulletin* with what I do for the school paper? They're two completely different things."

11 "Well, all I know is that everyone has to start somewhere, Tom. Even my brother Max did. He became a reporter by working his way up to it. I expect you'll have to do the same. Most of us do," cautioned his mother wisely.

12 "You're right, Mom. Besides, I have more important things to think about right now. I have quite a day facing me, so I'd better get started," sighed Tom, tossing back the covers and sliding out of bed. "Remember, Mrs. Hopple promised she'd take me downtown for my driver's test today so I can get my license. I can hardly wait."

13 "It will be very nice to have someone run errands for me when I'm tied up at work," said Mrs. Ellis.

14 "For a chance to drive, I'll go anywhere for you," laughed Tom, stumbling toward the bathroom.

15 "If you'll go anywhere, then go shower while I finish preparing breakfast," coaxed his mother.

Knowing the Words

Write the words from the story that have the meanings below.

1. meeting to get information

   <u>interview</u>
   (Par. 1)

2. news writer

   <u>journalist</u>
   (Par. 2)

3. wake up

   <u>rouse</u>
   (Par. 7)

In each row below, circle the three words that belong together.

4. (reporter) bakery (editor) (photographer)
5. (morning) (dawn) night (sunrise)
6. (school) (study) breakfast (classes)

Working with Words

Apostrophes are used to form **possessives,** words that show ownership. For example, *Tom's radio* means "the radio owned by Tom." Write possessives to complete the phrases.

Uncle Max   principal   alarm clock

1. the <u>alarm clock</u> loud buzzing
2. the <u>principal</u> newly painted office
3. <u>Uncle Max</u> electric typewriter

Use two words from each sentence below to form a compound word. Write the compound word in the blank.

4. The bud of a rose is a <u>rosebud</u>.
5. Work done at home is <u>homework</u>.
6. A walk near the side of a road is a

   <u>sidewalk</u>.

Reading and Thinking

1. For what newspaper does Uncle Max work?

   <u>The Kendall Bulletin</u>

2. Check the words that describe Tom.

   <u>✓</u> ambitious   <u>✗</u> lazy
   ____ unfriendly   <u>✓</u> enthusiastic

3. A **fact** is something that is known to be true. An **opinion** is what a person believes, but an opinion may or may not be true. Put **F** before the sentence that is a fact.

   <u>F</u> Men and women can be reporters.
   <u>✓</u> This is a good newspaper.

4. Do you think Tom will pass his driver's test? Give reasons for your answer. ____

   <u>Yes I do think he will pass his driving test</u>

Learning to Study

1. Imagine you wanted to know more about Uncle Max's job. Check the subjects you could look up in the encyclopedia.

   ____ trucks   <u>✓</u> editing
   <u>✓</u> newspapers   ____ cameras

2. Suppose you wanted to know more about driving a car. Check the subjects you would look up.

   ____ sunglasses   <u>✓</u> traffic signs
   <u>✓</u> traffic laws   ____ mountains

3. **Guide words** are the two words in dark print at the top of a dictionary page. Check the words that would appear on a dictionary page that had the guide words **interview-introduce.**

   <u>✓</u> into   ____ intruder
   ____ investigate   <u>✓</u> intestines

3

The Important Test

Read this story to see if Tom passes his driver's test.

1   Muttering to himself, Tom took another English muffin and <u>gulped</u> down a glass of orange juice.

2   "Are you talking to me?" asked Mrs. Ellis.

3   "Huh? Oh!" Then, pouring a glass of milk, he said, "I must have been talking to myself, Mom. I'm kind of worried about a math test I have this morning. And this afternoon, I've got to pass my driver's test. Meanwhile, I've got to finish my story about our shut-out football game. The problem is that I have an eight o'clock deadline."

4   "Tom, how many times have I spoken to you about leaving things until the last minute?"

5   "Don't say it, Mom, please. I know it's my own fault." With that, he hurried out of the house to catch his bus. His good-bye was muffled by the sound of the screen door slamming shut.

6   The day moved quickly for Tom, and finally it was time to meet Mrs. Hopple, his driver-education teacher.

7   "Are you ready to take the driving test?" asked Mrs. Hopple.

8   "As ready as I'll ever be," answered Tom. "The only thing that worries me is driving around those markers without hitting them."

9   "Just don't turn the wheel too sharply and you'll be OK. Most important of all, relax," advised his teacher.

10   "You make it sound so easy."

11   "Have confidence in yourself, Tom, and stop worrying. Just do what has to be done," said Mrs. Hopple encouragingly as she drove Tom downtown.

12   After Tom signed various forms, an examiner slid into the passenger seat. Getting behind the wheel, Tom felt nervous at the prospect of not passing the test.

13   "All right, Tom. Let's begin. Drive straight along this roadway until you come to the stop sign," instructed the examiner.

14   Tom went anxiously through the driving part of the test. The last thing he had to do was move the car into and out of a small space. His hands felt clammy as he drove between four markers that represented a narrow street. Then the examiner said, "Turn right," so Tom pulled up on the right side of a fifth marker.

15   "Did I do it OK?" Tom asked the examiner.

16   "Just continue," said the examiner, so Tom took a deep breath and put the car into reverse. His heart was pounding as he eased the car backward. He had to back around the fifth marker and between the four markers, ending up where he had started.

17   After stopping the car, Tom tried to catch his breath. Then the examiner congratulated him for passing the test!

Knowing the Words

Write the words from the story that have the meanings below.

1. possibility

_____
(Par. 12)

2. with an uneasy feeling

_____
(Par. 14)

3. stood for

_____
(Par. 14)

4. damp

_____
(Par. 14)

In each row below, circle the three words that belong together.

5. (car) (gasoline) (truck) backpack
6. (test) (exam) football (study)
7. (driver) muffin (pilot) (guide)

Working with Words

An ending that is added to a word to change its meaning or part of speech is called a **suffix.** The suffix **-ist** means "someone who does something." For example, the word *geologist* is "someone who studies geology." Add **-ist** to each word below. Then use the new word in a sentence.

1. organ _____

_____

2. cartoon _____

_____

The suffix **-ly** can be added to some words. For example, a person who talks in a loud way talks **loudly.** Find the word in paragraph 14 of the story that means "in an anxious way."

3. _____

Reading and Thinking

1. Check the main idea of the story.
____ waking up late
____ playing football
✓ Tom's driving test

Write the word that best completes each sentence.

2. Tom poured the _____ into the glass that was sitting on the counter.
bread   milk   ocean

3. We _____ that fifty people attended last week's football game.
confided   released   estimated

4. Why is Tom worried about passing his diving test? _____

_____

5. Find one sentence the author wrote to show how busy Tom's day was.

_____

_____

Learning to Study

Look at the chart and answer the questions.

Deadlines	Reporter	Department
May 4	Jenny	News
May 10	Christy	Art
May 12	Tom	Sports

1. Each deadline is in the month of __May__.

2. Who is the reporter for the sports page? __Tom__

3. Which reporter has the last deadline? __Tom__

A Success Story

Tom's busy day was a real winner! Read this story to find out why.

1 After Tom passed his driving test, Mrs. Hopple dropped him off at The Hideaway, the restaurant run by his mom since his dad's death two years before. Since it was after 4:00 P.M., the staff was setting up the tables for dinner. Tom rushed past them and into the back. He found his mother working in her office.

2 "Mom, I did it!" he shouted. The door slammed loudly behind him.

3 "Slow down, Tom, and start from the beginning," Mrs. Ellis laughed.

4 "Oh, I'm so excited, I can hardly think," said Tom. "First of all, Ms. Lopez was really impressed with my story. In fact, it's going on the front page! She said my writing style was clear and that my admiration for the athletes really showed through."

5 "Sounds a bit like your dream last night," remarked Mrs. Ellis.

6 "Yes, but that was a city newspaper, not a school paper," Tom reminded her.

7 "Don't tell me you've already forgotten what I said this morning. You have to start somewhere. And, besides, it looks to me as if you're off to an excellent start. I'm proud of you, Tom."

8 "Actually, you're right," grinned Tom. "You remember that math test I had to take this morning, don't you? Well, anyway, I think I did really well," Tom boasted.

9 "Good for you, Tom. I know how you struggle with it," she said sympathetically.

10 "Thanks, Mom. I can't wait to call Uncle Max and tell him. He gave me some study tips yesterday afternoon that were really helpful."

11 Then, leaning over, Tom whispered in his mother's ear. "Aren't you forgetting to ask me something?"

12 "My goodness, your story was accepted, and you did well on your math exam."

13 "And . . . ?"

14 "You did it, didn't you, Tom! You passed your driver's test just as I knew you would." Tom nodded, and his mother went on, "You're wrong if you think I forgot, though, Tom. I'd never forget something so important. I was just a little afraid to ask."

15 "Be afraid no more, Ma! This afternoon I became a licensed driver!" he crowed happily. "Do you want me to drive you home?" Tom asked enthusiastically.

16 "One step at a time," laughed Mrs. Ellis. "I won't be finished for another hour or so. But congratulations, Tom, I simply couldn't be happier for you."

Knowing the Words

Write the words from the story that have the meanings below.

1. workers

_____
(Par. 1)

2. great liking for

_____
(Par. 4)

3. people who play sports

_____
(Par. 4)

4. understandingly

_____
(Par. 9)

5. A **simile** is a figure of speech in which two unlike things are compared. Similes use the word *like* or *as*. For example, *as sly as a fox* is a simile. Write a simile to describe how Tom entered his mother's restaurant.

_____

_____

Working with Words

To form the possessive of a plural word that ends in *s*, add only an apostrophe. An example is *the girls' books*. Fill in each blank with the possessive form of the word in parentheses.

1. The _____ lunch order was taken by the headwaiter. (customers)

2. The _____ aprons were hung in the kitchen. (waiters)

3. The _____ tests were marked by the next day. (students)

4. The _____ stories were typed with word processors. (reporters)

Reading and Thinking

Write the word that best completes each sentence.

1. The _____ handed the girls a menu before seating them at a table.
reporter   server   teacher

2. The girl knew _____ where the birds' nest could be found.
cowardly   exactly   awfully

3. Number the events to show the order in which they happened.

____ Tom sees his mom at The Hideaway.

____ Tom takes his driving test.

____ Ms. Lopez praises Tom's story.

____ Mrs. Ellis congratulates Tom.

____ Mrs. Hopple drives Tom to The Hideaway.

4. Tom passed his math test because

_____.

5. Find one sentence the author wrote to show how Tom felt after his busy day.

_____

_____

Learning to Study

Write the name of the reference source that would provide the information needed.

atlas   thesaurus   almanac

1. Where could Betsy look to find out how much rain fell last year? _____

2. Where could Tom look to discover the location of the Black Hills? _____

3. Where could Jill look to find a synonym for the word *carve*? _____

7

Hopes Run High

As you read this story, you'll discover what Tom's next story will be.

1   It was Wednesday, and Tom just couldn't stop smiling when he arrived at school. Tom met his friend Betsy in the hall, and the two of them walked together to their journalism class.

2   "You sure look pleased with yourself," remarked Betsy.

3   "I am, Betsy, I am!" Tom grinned. "Do you remember how worried I was about that math exam?"

4   "You hardly talked about anything else for a week!" Betsy exclaimed.

5   "Well, I passed with a B+," he bragged.

6   "Hey, good for you, Tom!" she said, clapping him on the back. "I'm really happy for you, and I hear Ms. Lopez is putting your story about the football game on the front page. That must make you feel great!"

7   "It certainly does, Bets, but, believe it or not, there's more! You are now looking at a licensed driver."

8   "Wow!" she exclaimed, shaking Tom's hand. "That's really super! I can't wait to try for my driver's license, but I have to wait another eight months."

9   "Until then, Betsy, if you ever need a lift . . ."

10   "I'll know exactly whom to ask," she finished his sentence.

11   "I think my mom is pretty happy about it, too, because I can help run errands for her," Tom said.

12   "Knowing you, Tom, I'd say you'll be gulping down gallons of milk just so you can go to the grocery store for another carton," she teased.

13   "Hey, that's a good idea!" Tom laughed.

14   "You're something else," said Betsy, as they strolled into class.

15   "Good morning. How is everyone today?" asked Ms. Lopez, addressing her eleventh grade journalism class. "First let me tell you that I'm very pleased. Each of you met the deadline. All of your articles will appear in the next issue as planned."

16   Then Lance, a feature editor, raised his hand to ask a question. "Will we be discussing new assignments with our reporters and photographers today?"

17   "You certainly will, Lance," said Ms. Lopez, turning to the class. "As you know, the town will be holding its Fall Festival this weekend. I'd like some of you to cover it for our next edition. I'll give each of you your assignment, and if there are no other questions, you can use this time to discuss your next stories with your editors. I'll check with you tomorrow or the next day to see how your plans are going."

18   "I'm glad we're going to cover the Festival," Tom whispered to Betsy.

19   "And wait until you see my photos," she murmured back. "They'll put our story on the front page."

Knowing the Words

Write the words from the story that have the meanings below.

1. speaking to

   _____
   (Par. 15)

2. copy of a newspaper or magazine

   _____
   (Par. 15)

3. work given out

   _____
   (Par. 16)

Words with opposite meanings are called **antonyms.** Find an antonym in the story for each of these words.

4. frowning _____
   (Par. 1)

5. less _____
   (Par. 7)

6. ran _____
   (Par. 14)

7. all _____
   (Par. 17)

8. shouted _____
   (Par. 18)

Working with Words

The suffix **-able** means "able to." This suffix can be added to verbs to form adjectives. Form new words and write a sentence with each adjective.

1. break + able = _____

   _____

2. wash + able = _____

   _____

3. manage + able = _____

   _____

Reading and Thinking

Write the word that best completes each sentence.

1. The latest _____ of the paper will be delivered in the morning.
      issue   picture   journalism

2. The quarterback threw the _____ to the player in the end zone.
      light   story   ball

3. Where will Tom's football story appear in the paper? _____

4. Tom offered to give Betsy a ride whenever she needed it. Why? _____

   _____

5. Check the words that describe Betsy.
   ____ friendly   ____ supportive
   ____ nosy   ____ lazy

6. Check the main idea of paragraph 15.
   ____ Tom's journalism class
   ____ meeting the deadline
   ____ new assignments for the next issue

Learning to Study

The word you look up in a dictionary is called an **entry word.** All entry words are printed alphabetically in dark print down the left side of each column. Usually, an entry word is a base word. So if you want to know the meaning of *cities*, look for its base word, *city.* Next to each word below, write the entry word you would look for in the dictionary.

1. happier _____   3. liked _____

2. faster _____   4. slipping _____

A New Assignment

Read this story to learn more about the Fall Festival.

1   Impatiently, Tom and Betsy waited along with the other students to discuss their new assignments for the next edition of *The Knightly News,* the school newspaper.

2   "Now, I'd like to meet with Tom, Lance, and Betsy," said Ms. Lopez.

3   First addressing Tom, Ms. Lopez explained, "I would like you to cover the Fall Festival from a personal point of view. What do you think?"

4   "Gee, that's great!" blurted Tom. "Just tell me what you want and I'll do it."

5   "I know you will, Tom. Now just give me a minute to explain, and then Lance can take over."

6   "Sure, Ms. Lopez," Tom apologized.

7   "Tom, I've been quite pleased with your work lately. You've proven that you can put together a very good piece of writing if you put your mind to it."

8   Tom was so surprised, he could barely nod his head. Ms. Lopez continued, "Don't look so shocked. You have some talent, and I want you to use it to the best of your ability on this next assignment."

9   Lance continued, "As you know, the Festival is held at this time every year, and the proceeds go to help families in need. I want you to talk to some of those people. Find out how they feel. Unemployment is running high here since the factory closed. A lot of people are suffering."

10   "I think I understand. You want me to focus my attention on the people who need our help, not on the Festival itself," Tom said as he looked from Lance to Ms. Lopez.

11   "That's right, Tom," answered Ms. Lopez. "Some of the other reporters will be covering the activities at the fair. From you, I want something different, something special. I'm looking for an honest but thoughtfully written story. I want you to take a deeper look."

12   "You've got it, Ms. Lopez," answered Tom.

13   "Good! Lance, what do you have in mind for Betsy?" asked Ms. Lopez.

14   "You'll photograph some of the activities going on during the Festival," Lance began, "but the real focus will be the people at the Festival. Use your camera to capture their feelings. Then, I want you to take some shots of the Festival's organizers, because they're the heart of our community. Do you think you can handle it?"

15   "Are you kidding? It sounds great!" exclaimed Betsy, hugging her notebook.

16   Smiling, Ms. Lopez said, "Wonderful! Let's make this our best piece ever."

Knowing the Words

Write the words from the story that have the meanings below.

1. of a person

   _____
   (Par. 3)

2. said suddenly

   _____
   (Par. 4)

3. concentrate

   _____
   (Par. 10)

4. things to do

   _____
   (Par. 11)

5. Check the sentence in which *running* has the same meaning it does in paragraph 9.

   _____ Tracy saw the horse running through the wet field.

   _____ Beth was running the lawn mower.

   _____ Club attendance was running low due to heavy snow.

Find an antonym (opposite) in the story for each of these words.

6. last _____
   (Par. 3)

7. worst _____
   (Par. 8)

8. low _____
   (Par. 9)

Working with Words

A **prefix** is a group of letters added to the beginning of a word to change its meaning. The prefix **mid-** can mean "the middle part." For example, the word *midnight* means "the middle of the night." Add **mid-** to the word below. Use the new word in a sentence.

stream _____

_____

Reading and Thinking

1. Tom's school newspaper is named

   _____.

2. Tom and Betsy's next assignment is to

   cover the _____.

3. Check the main idea of paragraph 14.

   _____ helping families in need

   _____ photographing activities at the Festival

   _____ square dancing

4. Ms. Lopez praised Tom's work because

   _____

   _____.

Put **F** before the sentences that are facts. Put **O** before the sentences that are opinions.

5. _____ Everyone wants to be a reporter on a school newspaper.

6. _____ Photography is a fun hobby.

7. _____ There are many ways to earn money for special causes.

8. Do you think many citizens of Kendall will attend the Fall Festival? Why or why not?

   _____

   _____

Learning to Study

Beside each word below, write the entry word you would look for in the dictionary.

1. foxes _____ 4. clearly _____

2. walked _____ 5. steepest _____

3. hugged _____ 6. answered _____

Tom Learns a Lesson

Writing a newspaper story isn't easy. In this story, you'll discover why.

1 As Tom and Betsy walked out of their journalism class, they were deep in conversation. They were sharing their ideas and making plans for covering the Fall Festival together.

2 "I don't blame you for wanting to get started right away, Betsy, because I do, too. I don't want to rush this one just because I put it off too long. Sometimes I do."

3 "You allow yourself a little time to rework your writing, too, don't you?" asked Betsy.

4 "I like to let it sit for a day. Then I take another look at it. That's my method."

5 "I'd do the same thing if I knew Ms. Lopez would be looking at it. I've seen her reject a lot of stories," said Betsy. "Maybe we can work on some of this together, Tom. If we do it right, this story is going to interest a lot of people."

6 The day of the Festival finally came. Betsy hurried about taking pictures. In the meantime, Tom talked to a number of the Festival's organizers.

7 Tom left the Festival late in the day. Returning home, he began writing his story for the paper, using the notes he'd taken earlier in the day. After many rewrites, he was pleased with his story. On Sunday, Betsy came over. The two of them shared their work.

8 The next day, Tom met Betsy at her locker. She said, "I think Ms. Lopez will really like our work."

9 "I hope so," answered Tom uncertainly. He felt his confidence slowly sinking like a ship in the water.

10 "Well, she won't be disappointed today!" Betsy exclaimed. "Come on," said Betsy as they walked bravely into journalism class.

11 Ms. Lopez reviewed the material they had handed to her. Then she said, "The photos are good, Betsy. Now we need to decide which ones we want to print." Then turning to Tom, Ms. Lopez continued, "However, Tom, I believe something is missing from your article. The piece is flat. You've told me that the people are grateful, but from an outsider's point of view."

12 "Hmm . . . I didn't think of that. I guess I wrote it as someone who has everything he needs. Maybe my story could have more feeling for the people who benefit from the Festival."

13 "I'm glad you see my point, Tom. Write the article again, and we'll talk about it."

14 "It will be on your desk first thing tomorrow morning," promised Tom, as he turned to leave.

Knowing the Words

Write the words from the story that have the meanings below.

1. way of doing something

_____
(Par. 4)

2. turn down

_____
(Par. 5)

3. receive help

_____
(Par. 12)

4. What is the simile in paragraph 9?

_____

_____

5. Circle the three words that belong together.

festival   parade

cocoons   games

6. A **synonym** is a word with the same or nearly the same meaning as another word. Check the sets of words that are synonyms.

_____ ideas—thoughts

_____ now—immediately

_____ day—night

_____ like—enjoy

Working with Words

Rewrite each group of words below. Use possessive forms.

1. the story belonging to Tom

_____

2. the cameras belonging to the men

_____

Reading and Thinking

1. Number the events to show the order in which they happened,

_____ Ms. Lopez praises Betsy's photos.

_____ Tom writes his story about the Festival.

_____ Tom and Betsy attend the Festival.

_____ Betsy goes to Tom's home.

_____ Tom and Betsy discuss their assignment.

2. Check each word or phrase that describes Ms. Lopez.

_____ careless

_____ helpful

_____ expects the best from her students

3. Check two headlines that might have appeared in *The Knightly News* during the Fall Festival.

_____ Flood Destroys Kendall

_____ Festival Parade Watched by 2,000

_____ Students Cover Fall Festival

4. Tom was very nervous when it was time to turn in his story. Find one sentence the author wrote to show how Tom felt.

_____

_____

Learning to Study

The signs below were used to help Kendall's visitors locate helpful services. Match the signs in the left column with the services they stand for in the right column.

1. _____ ✚   **a.** Information

2. _____ 🍴   **b.** Telephone

3. _____ ⊘   **c.** Baggage Check-In

4. _____ ☏   **d.** First Aid

5. _____ 🧳   **e.** Restaurant

13

Tom Joins Uncle Max

In this story, Tom catches a glimpse of the workings at a newspaper firm.

1   "That was quite a story you wrote about the Fall Festival, Tom," complimented Uncle Max. "It had feeling."

2   "Thanks, Uncle Max," answered Tom thoughtfully.

3   "If you don't mind, I'd like to show it to my editor," said Uncle Max.

4   "Mind? Are you kidding?"

5   "It's my pleasure," said Uncle Max as he carefully looked at his nephew. "Who knows? Maybe your story will appear in *The Kendall Bulletin.*"

6   Looking at his feet, Tom thanked Uncle Max again. Noting his nephew's embarrassment, Uncle Max quickly changed the subject by asking, "Are we still on for Saturday's homecoming game?"

7   "Sure!" Tom answered. "Mom, especially, is looking forward to it. She's even going to take the day off. Are you covering the game for the *Bulletin* again this year?"

8   "I certainly am," answered Uncle Max. "It's one of my favorite assignments. It gives me a chance to see some old friends and to have a good time while I'm doing my job."

9   The day of the homecoming game finally arrived. Tom, his sister Meg, and Mrs. Ellis piled into Uncle Max's station wagon, setting off for an evening of cheering and meeting old friends. They shouted until they were hoarse. And, happy that Kendall High's team won, they headed for home.

10   As they pulled up in front of the Ellis house, Uncle Max said, "Say, Tom, I have to file my piece on today's game. How about keeping me company?"

11   "If it's all right with Mom . . . ?"

12   "Just don't stay out late, you two," Mrs. Ellis laughed as she and Meg climbed out of the car.

13   It is said that a newspaper never sleeps. Sure enough, the newsroom was bustling with noise when Tom and Uncle Max arrived. Despite the lateness of the hour, a number of reporters were still working at their desks. Still others were scurrying around the room.

14   While Uncle Max worked, Tom wandered around the different departments. Finally, he went to see where the paper was printed. The presses were ready to roll. The delivery trucks were pulling up outside. They were ready to be loaded with the Sunday edition. Tom had seen so much that his head was swimming.

15   "Sort of takes your breath away, doesn't it?" asked Uncle Max, coming up beside Tom. "By the way, my editor would like to run your Fall Festival story in tomorrow's edition of the *Bulletin*—with your permission, of course."

16   "My permission? I can't believe it!" Tom exclaimed. "Of course you can print it. Just wait until Mom sees it," Tom crowed.

Knowing the Words

Write the words from the story that have the meanings below.

1. praised

_____
(Par. 1)

2. shy or uncomfortable feeling

_____
(Par. 6)

3. in spite of

_____
(Par. 13)

4. Check the sentence in which *off* has the same meaning it does in paragraph 7.

_____ Because I hadn't practiced for many weeks, my golf game was off.

_____ Please turn off the lights when you finish.

_____ We all had some time off because the circus was in town.

Homophones are words that sound alike but have different meanings. Circle the homophone with the correct meaning in each sentence below.

5. Meg wants to go with Uncle Max (too, two).

6. It took an (our, hour) for the bus to arrive with the athletes.

Working with Words

The prefix **re-** means "again." The prefix **pre-** means "before." Read the clues. Add **re-** or **pre-** to each underlined word to form a word that matches the clue.

1. to <u>test</u> before _____

2. to <u>write</u> again _____

3. to <u>paint</u> again _____

4. before a <u>game</u> _____

Reading and Thinking

1. Check the main idea of the story.

_____ a great football game

_____ Tom's visit to the *Bulletin*

_____ newspaper deadlines

2. A **summary** briefly expresses information about a topic. To summarize, you must find the most important information and put it in an order that makes sense. Read paragraph 13 from the story. Summarize the important information of the paragraph in one sentence.

_____

_____

3. Why do you think the *Bulletin* reporters were working late at night?

_____

_____

4. The *Bulletin* newsroom was very busy when Tom and Uncle Max arrived. Find one sentence the author wrote to show

how busy it really was. _____

_____

_____

5. Do you think Tom will ever have another story printed in the *Bulletin*?

Why or why not? _____

Learning to Study

A newspaper **caption** is a one- or two-sentence explanation of a newspaper photo. It usually appears under the photo. Write a caption for the photo of the football game.

_____

_____

The King of Escape

How can a front-page story change a person's life?

1. "Please listen carefully as Tom gives his report," Ms. Lopez began. "Tom, you may begin your report on the importance of a front-page story."

2. "It was 1898," Tom began. "A young man raced up the stairs of a Chicago apartment house. Once inside, he spread the morning paper on the table. The front-page picture showed him smiling. At his side were the police chief and two jail guards. The story went like this:

3. **Young Magician Slips Out of Jail**

   A twenty-four-year-old magician named Harry Houdini boasts that no locks, chains, or jails can hold him. He has proved his claim. Houdini asked the head of a Chicago jail to lock him in a cell.

4. Guards checked to see that Houdini did not have any sharp instruments on his person. The guards put handcuffs on him and then locked him in an old cell.

5. Ten minutes later, Houdini walked into the jail's main office. What's more, he entered the office through the front door. The police chief and the guards stood and stared at Houdini in amazement. They could not explain the young magician's escape.

6. "This front-page story made Houdini famous," Tom said. "For years he had invited reporters to watch his act. He had wanted the publicity. During this time, he and his wife Bess worked as a team. They played in small theaters, circuses, and traveling shows across the land. They might put on ten shows a day, but only make twenty-five dollars a week. Often the team had no work at all.

7. "After the newspaper story, Houdini began to get offers to perform from all over the world. In England, he was handcuffed and chained with twenty pounds of iron. The magician was then tossed into a river. He swam to the surface in less than a minute.

8. "Russian police locked him in a small cell used to carry prisoners. It was really a small, strong steel safe on wheels. No one had ever escaped from it. Houdini freed himself in forty-five minutes.

9. "In Washington, D.C., Houdini's arms were tied, and he was lifted one hundred feet into the air, head down. In less than three minutes, he was free!" Tom exclaimed. "The crowd below cheered as the straps fell to the ground.

10. "For years, Houdini proved his word. Nothing could hold him down. He escaped drowning two thousand times, he picked more than twelve thousand locks, and he could free himself from traps specially made to hold him. Houdini no longer had to beg reporters to watch his act. They gladly went to write about the 'King of Escape.'"

Knowing the Words

Write the words from the story that have the meanings below.

1. brags

    _____
    (Par. 3)

2. statement made as a fact

    _____
    (Par. 3)

3. public attention

    _____
    (Par. 6)

4. Check the phrase in which *slip* has the same meaning as it does in the newspaper headline in paragraph 3.

    ____ a small piece of paper

    ____ to lose balance

    ____ to move quietly or easily

Working with Words

Rewrite each group of words below. Use possessive forms.

1. the handcuffs of the guards _____

    _____

2. the escape of Houdini _____

    _____

The prefix **ir-** usually means "not." Add **ir-** to each word below. Then use the new word in a sentence.

3. responsible _____

    _____

4. resistible _____

    _____

5. regular _____

    _____

Reading and Thinking

1. Check the main idea of the story.

    ____ traveling around the world

    ____ an amazing escape artist

    ____ how to perform magic tricks

2. What did people think of Houdini's acts before the front-page story?

    _____

    _____

3. How did the front-page story change

    Houdini's life? _____

    _____

    _____

4. The author wrote this story to

    ____ talk about traveling.

    ____ explain Houdini's childhood.

    ____ explain the effects of a newspaper story.

5. Write one change in Houdini's life after

    the newspaper story was printed. _____

    _____

Learning to Study

Complete the following outline to explain what happened to Houdini in each place.

I. England

   A. Handcuffed and chained

   B. _____

   C. _____

II. Russia

   A. _____

   B. _____

Moving Day

Have you ever moved? Read this story to find out about a very unusual moving day.

1   Betsy was excited one day when she came to school. "Tom, my family is moving next week! Maybe you could write a story about our moving day for the school paper," she said.

2   Tom stared at Betsy and asked, "Where are you moving, and aren't you upset about leaving?"

3   Betsy just smiled and said, "Oh, we're only moving about three blocks from where we live now. My family isn't moving to a different house. Our house is moving to a new location!"

4   "That is really different," Tom remarked. "But why are you going to move in the first place?"

5   "The new highway the state is building will cut right through our yard," Betsy explained. "Everyone in my family likes our house so much that we didn't want to find another one. We decided to have the house moved. Our new lot is on the corner of Fifth and Broad Streets."

6   Tom learned that Mr. and Mrs. Davis, Betsy's parents, had to obtain a permit for the house to be transported on city streets. At the new site, a basement had been dug for the Davis house. It was ready for the house to be placed above it. Before the move, the utility companies came. They disconnected the water, gas, and electricity. Then, the family had to pack and take out of the house anything that was fragile.

7   At last, all these jobs were done. On Friday morning, the house-moving firm came with all its tools. Betsy snapped pictures of the whole process. First, the six-person crew jacked up the house almost the same way a car is jacked up to change a tire. They placed cylinder-shaped beams under the house. Then they rolled the house very slowly onto a flatbed truck. When the house was on the truck, a police escort arrived.

8   The police rode on motorcycles in front of the truck. Betsy and her family followed in their car. The house was almost the same width as the street on which it traveled! The truck went very slowly as the people on Fifth Street stared in wonder. They couldn't believe that a house was moving down their street.

9   When the truck arrived at the new site, the crew slowly moved the house back onto the cylinder-shaped beams and rolled it off the truck. They then placed the house over the new basement.

10   The entire house-moving process took about twelve days to complete. Betsy came into class the Monday after the move. "At last we have all our furniture and dishes back in their right places. It seems the only thing that has changed is our address," she laughed.

18

Knowing the Words

Write the words from the story that have the meanings below.

1. gas, water, or electric service

_____
(Par. 6)

2. roller-shaped

_____
(Par. 7)

3. thick pieces of wood

_____
(Par. 7)

4. **Abbreviations** are shortened forms of words. Write this address without abbreviations.

Dr. Trina Davis
319 Oak St.
New York, NY 10012

_____

_____

_____

Learning to Study

Complete this outline.

I. Things that were done before moving day

A. _____

B. _____

C. _____

D. _____

II. Things that were done on moving day

A. _____

B. _____

C. _____

D. _____

Reading and Thinking

1. Number of events to show the order in which they happened.

_____A basement was dug for the house.

_____The crew rolled the house to a flatbed truck using cylinders.

_____The crew began to raise up the house using jacks.

_____Mr. and Mrs. Davis obtained a permit.

_____Betsy returned to class on Monday.

2. Why did Mr. and Mrs. Davis have to get a permit? _____

_____

3. Why did the family have to remove from the house anything that was fragile?

_____

_____

4. Why was the house moved onto cylinder-shaped beams? _____

_____

5. The main idea of paragraph 8 is

_____ .

Working with Words

Sometimes suffixes are added to verbs to form nouns. Write the noun that is formed from each verb and suffix.

	Verb	Suffix	Noun
1.	depend	ence	_____
2.	correct	ion	_____
3.	forgive	ness	_____

19

A Month Without the Paper

Read this story to learn the importance of the newspaper in a community.

1   It was a sunny morning. Tom and his mother were enjoying a brisk walk around the block. All at once a thought occurred to Tom.

2   "Mom, I think I have a topic for my speech class assignment. Remember a few years ago when the newspaper companies in Fairlawn went on strike?"

3   "Of course, I remember, Tom," his mother answered. "Why do you ask?"

4   "Well," Tom began, "things were different without the newspaper. Why couldn't I give my speech about some of the differences?"

5   "That's an interesting topic," Mrs. Ellis answered. "Where would you begin?"

6   "I guess I'll start by talking to some people from Fairlawn to see what they remember. I'll see if Uncle Max will introduce me to some of his friends in Fairlawn."

7   The next day, Tom and Uncle Max drove to Fairlawn to visit a friend of Uncle Max.

8   "Tom, this is Lynn Mills," said Uncle Max when they arrived at Lynn's house. "Tom and I were hoping you could tell us a little about the newspaper strike a few years ago."

9   "I'll tell you what I remember," said Lynn. "Some of my friends read the morning newspaper at breakfast or on their way to their jobs. Then the newspaper company shut down. They had to change their routines. Many readers thought it would be easy to do without the paper. In fact, I thought I could just listen to the news on the radio or television," Lynn continued. "I didn't realize how many different things newspapers have to offer."

10   "What do you mean?" Tom asked uncertainly. Lynn stopped to think.

11   She told Tom that on Friday night, she didn't have the paper's entertainment section. "I didn't know what shows or movies were in town. I called five theaters before I found a movie I wanted to see," Lynn said. "And on Saturday when I went grocery shopping, my bill was higher than usual. I hadn't been able to clip any coupons from the paper all week."

12   "How did people feel as the strike wore on?" asked Uncle Max.

13   "The strike had an effect on the entire city," Lynn replied. "Couples had become engaged and married. The announcements were not in the paper. Some people weren't aware of an acquaintance's death because they hadn't been able to read the paper."

14   "What happened once the strike was settled?" Tom asked.

15   "After a month, the strike was finally settled. Everyone was quite happy," Lynn answered. "Most of us had never realized how much we depended on the paper for news and entertainment."

16   As Tom and Uncle Max prepared to leave, Tom thanked Lynn. "You've been very helpful. I'm glad we had a chance to talk."

Knowing the Words

Write the words from the story that have the meanings below.

1. lively

_____
(Par. 1)

2. came to mind

_____
(Par. 1)

3. stopping work for a special purpose

_____
(Par. 2)

4. a person you know

_____
(Par. 13)

Find the synonom (word with similar meaning) in the story for each of these words.

5. part _____
(Par. 11)

6. film _____
(Par. 11)

7. friend _____
(Par. 13)

Learning to Study

Read this newspaper coupon and answer the questions.

Lister's Limeade	One coupon per purchase
OFFER GOOD	
15¢ September 16–21 15¢	

1. If you used this newspaper coupon, how much money would you save? _____

2. Could you use this coupon on September 30? Why or why not?

_____

_____

Reading and Thinking

1. The main idea of paragraph 9 is

____ entertainment in Fairlawn.

____ the strike's effects.

____ saving money.

2. The author wrote this story to

____ talk about strikes.

____ explain newspaper advertising.

____ explain the importance of a newspaper.

3. Write two effects the newspaper strike had on the people of Fairlawn.

_____

_____

_____

4. What might have happened if the strike had lasted longer than a month?

_____

_____

_____

Working with Words

Write the compound word from the list that makes sense in each sentence.

footsteps   suitcases   sidewalk

1. Jean and I arrived at the airport

without our _____.

2. As I was walking into the shop, I heard

_____ behind me.

3. Shoppers had a hard time walking on

the snow-covered _____.

Backpacking in Yosemite

Read this story to learn more about mountain climbing in Yosemite National Park.

1   "Some of you have asked me how I got interested in journalism," Ms. Lopez said one day. "Let me tell you about one of my first jobs.

2   "When I was in college," Ms. Lopez went on, "I worked for a small newspaper each summer. One story was on mountain climbing. The city editor, Ann, gave it to Liz, a senior reporter, and Kim, a staff photographer. I joined them. My job would be to put the beauty of the climb on paper.

3   "It was Liz's plan to go on a mountain climbing trip to Yosemite National Park. The park lies in the Sierra Nevada. It's two hundred miles east of San Francisco.

4   "We left for the park on a Saturday morning. After hiking for a few hours, we came to a large meadow. To our right, we could see a beautiful waterfall. We decided to set up camp there. Kim took some photos. The scenery was breathtaking.

5   "Liz and Kim put up our tents. After supper, we watched a grand sunset and then got some rest before the more challenging part of our trip.

6   "In the morning, Kim took a photo of a magnificent rainbow near the waterfall. She also took pictures of two deer grazing quietly some distance from the tents," Ms. Lopez said.

7   "The three of us started again on our hike. As we moved through the silent forests, the climb became steeper and much colder. The mountain air was as cold as ice!" Ms. Lopez exclaimed.

8   "We put on the snowshoes we had brought for the final part of the journey. The broad tracks of our snowshoes were the only marks on the smooth snow.

9   "By early afternoon, the top of the

mountain was in sight. The wind suddenly picked up, swirling snow around us. The last few steps seemed more than our muscles could bear.

10   "Silently, we stood in awe at the top of the mountain. Together we looked down at the valley. It was a magnificent sight. I could've stayed there for hours, but Liz thought we should start back before the snow could cover our tracks.

11   "The three of us wearily descended the mountain. Before we got back to our camp, we looked once more at the snow-covered mountain.

12   "Just think," Ms. Lopez said to the class, "we made it to the top of that mountain. The paper's readers enjoyed the story about our climb, and I knew right then that teaching students to write about beautiful places and interesting topics was what I wanted to do."

Knowing the Words

Write the words from the story that have the meanings below.

1. beautiful sights

   _____
   (Par. 4)

2. exciting, thrilling

   _____
   (Par. 4)

3. demanding

   _____
   (Par. 5)

4. came down

   _____
   (Par. 11)

5. What is the simile in paragraph 7?

   _____

   _____

Circle the word with the correct meaning in each sentence below.

6. May I have a (piece, peace) of watermelon?

7. Did you see the large (bear, bare) that stood near the foot of the mountain?

8. Carla likes to (read, reed) the newspaper when she wakes up in the morning.

Learning to Study

Entry words are divided into syllables. This shows where the words can be divided at the end of a line of writing. Divide these words into syllables.

1. v a l l e y
2. w o r k i n g
3. m o u n t a i n
4. s i l e n t
5. b e a u t i f u l
6. n e w s p a p e r
7. m u s c l e s
8. t o p i c s
9. s u m m e r
10. c o l l e g e

Reading and Thinking

Write the word that best completes each sentence.

1. Ann painted the _____ yesterday.
   journey   sound   scenery

2. The goats _____ the cliff.
   propped   descended   suggested

3. How did the words *beautiful waterfall, silent forests,* and *deer grazing quietly* make you feel?

   ____ tired   ____ upset   ____ peaceful

4. Where is Yosemite National Park?

   _____

5. Ms. Lopez and the others wore

   snowshoes because _____

   _____.

6. Do you think Ms. Lopez will go mountain climbing again? Why or why not?

   _____

Working with Words

The suffix **-ation** means "state, condition, action, or process of." For example, the word *presentation* means "the act of presenting." Add **-ation** to each word. Then use the new word in a sentence. You may have to drop the final *e* before adding the suffix.

1. expect _____

   _____

2. imagine _____

   _____

3. reserve _____

   _____

In the News

Read this story to learn how Tom plans to write his next story.

1   Tom opened one eye. He shut it at once against the sunlight that was streaming in through his bedroom window. Groaning, he rolled over and planted his feet firmly on the floor.

2   Tom had had such a great time with Uncle Max the night before, he'd nearly forgotten about the school band's baked goods sale he would be covering that day. He started to think about the day's schedule. Suddenly a thought came to him. Tom came bounding down the stairs like a speeding locomotive and almost crashed into his mother. "Mom, where's today's paper? I've got to show you something incredible!"

3   "It must still be on the front porch, Tom. I haven't brought it in yet," his mother answered.

4   Tom brought the paper in and sat at the kitchen table. Searching through the paper, he finally came to the "Community Interest" section. There, just as Uncle Max had promised, was Tom's Fall Festival article.

5   "I'm very proud of you, Tom," said Mrs. Ellis as she leaned over Tom's shoulder.

6   "Thanks, Mom," Tom said. "Ms. Lopez helped me see that focusing on the families in need was the best way to write this story. I think I'll use the same approach when I cover the band members' bake sale."

7   "What do you mean?" asked Meg as she joined Tom at the table.

8   "Well, I want to write the story from a band member's point of view. Maybe I can find out how a person gets started playing in the band," Tom said.

9   "The band must feel really proud when they perform, especially after all those hours of practice," Mrs. Ellis suggested. "Maybe you could put that in your story."

10   "That's a good idea," Tom agreed.

11   "What time are we supposed to meet the band members?" Mrs. Ellis asked.

12   "I told them to meet us at The Hideaway at ten o'clock so we'd have time to get the bake sale set up before your customers start arriving," Tom answered.

13   "Then we'd better get going. Come on, Meg. I'll drop you off at Kate's on our way."

14   When Tom and his mother finally arrived at The Hideaway, several band members were already there. They decided to set up the tables in the restaurant's lobby. Soon the place was jammed with customers. The restaurant's Sunday buffet was now famous. Everything from waffles to ham salad was served.

15   Tom watched happily as the baked goods disappeared. It looked like the bake sale would be a success. The band members would look great in their new uniforms each time they marched onto the field. And after talking with some of the band members, Tom knew he would have no trouble writing his story.

Knowing the Words

Write the words from the story that have the meanings below.

1. unbelievable

_____
(Par. 2)

2. meal in which diners serve themselves

_____
(Par. 14)

3. crisp batter cakes

_____
(Par. 14)

Check the three words in each column that belong together.

4. ____ band   **5.** ____ breakfast

____ parade   ____ juice

____ football game   ____ porch

____ science   ____ pancakes

6. What is the simile in paragraph 2?

_____

_____

7. Check the sentence in which *planted* has the same meaning it does in paragraph 1.

____ Jean planted four rows of cucumbers.

____ Jo planted her feet in the dirt before swinging the bat.

Learning to Study

Complete the following outline.

I. Playing in a Band
   A. Playing well requires practice.
   B. _____

II. Choosing a Musical Instrument
   A. Some instruments are expensive.
   B. _____

Reading and Thinking

Write the word that best completes each sentence.

1. Melissa _____ a carton of milk.
   suggested   opened   crashed

2. The rain _____ against the window, making it hard to see.
   splashed   talked   decided

3. In which section of the paper did Tom's story appear? _____

4. Number the events to show the order in which they happened.

____ Tom and his mom arrive at The Hideaway.

____ Tom reads his story aloud.

____ Customers arrive at the restaurant.

____ Mrs. Ellis takes Meg to Kate's house.

____ Tom wakes from sleeping.

5. The band members will be able to buy new uniforms because _____

_____ .

Working with Words

The prefix **in-** sometimes means "not" or "the opposite of." Write words that have the following meanings by adding the prefix **in-** to a base word. Then use the new word in a sentence.

1. not correct _____

_____

2. not direct _____

_____

Playing to Win

What might Meg and Kate see if they go to the tri-city competition in Philadelphia?

1 Tom drove slowly out of The Hideaway's parking lot. Soon, he had picked up Meg and Kate from gymnastics. Tom then headed for home.

2 "What's in the box, Tom?" asked Meg, as she climbed the steps of their porch.

3 "Just what two future Olympic athletes need after a hard practice," he answered. Then, sharing the muffins he'd bought at the bake sale, he asked, "How was practice?"

4 Rubbing her ankle, Meg said, "I fell a few times, but Mr. Lee, our new coach, helped me see what I was doing wrong."

5 "He said she was trying too hard," Kate added.

6 "Mr. Lee showed me that I was gripping the bar too tightly. I couldn't push off smoothly, so my dismounts were too rough," said Meg.

7 "It's hard to relax, though, knowing the area competition is only a few weeks away," Kate sighed.

8 "Don't get discouraged," Mrs. Ellis said as she entered the room. "I know you two are going to do just fine."

9 "We've got to do better than just fine, Mom," said Meg firmly. "We want to go to the tri-city competition in Philadelphia. So we have to win either first or second place."

10 "Have you ever been to Philadelphia?" Kate asked Mrs. Ellis.

11 "My brother took me there with him on a business trip once. We thoroughly enjoyed the City of Brotherly Love. There was so much to see."

12 "Did you see the Liberty Bell?" Kate asked Mrs. Ellis.

13 "Yes, I did. I saw it before it was moved to the Liberty Bell Pavilion where it now hangs. The bell used to be called the Old State House Bell or Old Independence."

14 "I remember reading once," Tom began, "that the Liberty Bell weighs more than two thousand pounds. Do you know when it was made, Mom?"

15 "It was made in England in 1752. I think the province of Pennsylvania paid about three hundred dollars for it."

16 "What else did you see when you were there?" Kate asked.

17 "One place I'll never forget was Philadelphia's Italian Market. It was an outdoor market stretching block after block, where you could buy everything from apples to live chickens!"

18 "It sounds neat!"

19 "I hope you girls have a chance to see Philadelphia for yourselves next month," Mrs. Ellis said.

20 "We're sure going to try," replied Meg.

Photograph courtesy of Philadelphia Convention & Visitors Bureau

Knowing the Words

Write the words from the story that have the meanings below.

1. contest between people or teams

   _____
   (Par. 7)

2. open building used for shelter

   _____
   (Par. 13)

3. main division of a country

   _____
   (Par. 15)

Find antonyms (opposites) in the story for each of these words.

4. quickly _____
   (Par. 1)

5. easy _____
   (Par. 3)

6. loosely _____
   (Par. 6)

7. forget _____
   (Par. 14)

8. Write this address without abbreviations.

   Mr. Luke Logan
   261 Washington St.
   Philadelphia, PA 19106

   _____

   _____

   _____

Working with Words

Fill in each blank with the possessive form of the word in parentheses.

1. The _____ new tennis racket was a gift from her students. (coach)

2. The _____ awards were placed in the trophy case. (athletes)

3. My _____ coach flew to the track meet. (sister)

Reading and Thinking

1. Check the main idea of paragraph 13.

   _____ becoming a gymnast

   _____ a visit to Philadelphia

   _____ the Liberty Bell

Put **F** before the sentences that are facts.
Put **O** before the sentences that are opinions.

2. _____ Gymnastics is the most graceful sport.

3. _____ The Liberty Bell weighs more than two thousand pounds.

4. _____ Philadelphia is a great place.

5. Summarize the important information of paragraph 9 in one sentence.

   _____

   _____

6. Why did Meg rub her ankle after gymnastics practice? _____

   _____

7. The author wrote this story to

   _____ describe Philadelphia.

   _____ talk about gymnastics.

   _____ describe Meg's coach, Mr. Lee.

Learning to Study

Write the number of the encyclopedia volume that would have the most information for each of the topics below.

Vol. 1	Vol. 2	Vol. 3	Vol. 4	Vol. 5	Vol. 6	Vol. 7
A–C	D–F	G–J	K–M	N–Q	R–T	U–Z

1. The Liberty Bell _____

2. Independence Hall _____

3. The population of Pennsylvania _____

27

The Workout

What does it take to be an Olympic champion? Read this story and find out.

1 "I'm going to watch Meg work out today," Tom reminded his mother one day. "She's promised to introduce me to Mr. Lee."

2 "Meg, do you really think you should be working out on that ankle today?" asked Mrs. Ellis.

3 "It feels fine, now, Mom," Meg said. "Besides, I can't afford to miss this practice session. The competition in Philadelphia is only a few weeks away."

4 As they left the house, Mrs. Ellis couldn't help calling after them, "Be careful, dear."

5 Soon they arrived at the gym. Meg introduced Tom to her new coach. Then she went to warm up on the balance beam with the other gymnasts.

6 "It always amazes me that someone can perform such breathtaking movements on that rail. It's only four inches wide!" Tom remarked.

7 "Yes," said Mr. Lee, "performing on the balance beam is very difficult. That's why, when I find someone as talented as Meg, I work her so hard. She can be on the U.S. Olympic team, but she must be determined."

8 Meg gracefully raised her legs and did a shoulder stand on the beam. Tom said admiringly, "She makes it look so easy."

9 "That is part of her talent. She combines balance with flexibility," explained her coach. "She is even more in control when she's on the uneven parallel bars."

10 "What about her ankle?" asked Tom.

11 "She must be particularly careful with her dismounts. In other words, she must lower herself gently to the floor, rather than simply jump off the beam."

12 "But will she?" he asked uncertainly.

13 "Certainly, she will! She wants to go to Philadelphia, so she won't do anything foolish, believe me."

14 Tom replied, "You're right, of course."

15 "Are you an athlete?" Mr. Lee asked.

16 "Well, I wouldn't go that far, but I do run on the track team. I lack the dedication it takes, though, to be a real athlete like Meg," Tom admitted.

17 As they spoke, Meg bent forward. She kicked one leg up behind her. Then, reaching down, she gripped the balance beam with both hands. Raising her other leg, she pulled herself up into an English handstand.

18 A poster with the motto of the Olympic Games—Swifter, Higher, Stronger—caught Tom's eye. "Go for it, Meg," he whispered.

Knowing the Words

Write the words from the story that have the meanings below.

1. class

_____
(Par. 3)

2. without full strength

_____
(Par. 11)

3. devotion

_____
(Par. 16)

Match each word with its abbreviation.

4. ____ Street   **a.** U. S.

5. ____ Pennsylvania   **b.** Mr.

6. ____ United States   **c.** St.

7. ____ Mister   **d.** PA

Working with Words

Rewrite each group of words below. Use possessive forms.

1. the towel that is used by the gymnast

_____

2. the covers of the books

_____

3. the game that belongs to Meg

_____

4. the field that is used by the players

_____

5. the green and white stripes of the flags

_____

6. the whistle that belongs to Tom

_____

Reading and Thinking

1. How do you know Meg is determined to become a star athlete?

_____

_____

2. Check the words that describe Mr. Lee.

____ caring   ____ surprised

____ sad   ____ wise

Put **F** before the sentences that are facts. Put **O** before the sentences that are opinions.

3. ____ A gymnast needs good balance.

4. ____ Gymnastics is a difficult sport.

5. ____ The balance beam is about four inches wide.

6. ____ Gymnastics is the most graceful sport.

7. Do you think Meg will attend the competition in Philadelphia? Why or

why not? _____

_____

_____

Learning to Study

Complete this partial outline.

I. The Problems of Being a Gymnast
    A. Many hours of practice

    B. _____

    C. _____

Check the subjects you could look up in the encyclopedia if you wanted to know more about gymnastics.

____ physical fitness   ____ Olympic Games

____ racing   ____ tie-dyeing

29

Meeting Dr. Stevens

As you read, you'll discover the steps that scientists use to test a theory.

1 After school one day, Tom and Betsy sat in the library. They were waiting to interview Dr. Kay Stevens. She was a professor at the local college and was going to be a judge for the school science fair.

2 "Do you know what you want to ask her?" inquired Betsy. "I think we should get some background on her. You know, ask her things like what prompted her interest in science and what university she attended."

3 "I want to talk to her about her career," suggested Tom. "Then we can concentrate on what's happening in research today. What do you think?"

4 "That sounds good. We can wrap it up by getting her thoughts on next week's science fair."

5 "That's a great idea, since everyone is so excited about this year's fair," said Tom. "The projects are always so amazing. There's Dr. Stevens now," said Tom, pointing toward the entrance.

6 They rose to thank Dr. Stevens for meeting with them and sat down to begin their interview. Tom and Betsy learned about her interests and career. Then Tom asked Dr. Stevens to talk about current research in science.

7 "The great thing about science is that it never stays the same," she began. "What's science fiction today will be ours tomorrow to enjoy. For instance, when I was young, we watched Flash Gordon travel through space. We knew, though, that space travel could never happen," she said, smiling. "Well, now we've been to the moon and back. It's the same in many fields of science.

8 "But, you know," she went on, "in all fields of science, the same steps are followed. First, a scientist develops an idea, or theory. Next, experiments are done to test it. Later, the findings are studied. Only then can any conclusions be drawn."

9 "Why did you choose to be a science fair judge?" Betsy asked.

10 Dr. Stevens answered, "These science fairs are so important. They give our students a chance to test and prove their theories and, of course, to share their projects. The ideas they dream of today will benefit us tomorrow."

11 When she left, Betsy turned to Tom and remarked, "I've never really liked science, you know. Dr. Stevens, though, has helped me think about it in a whole new way."

12 "I know what you mean, Betsy," Tom said. "I've got to try to capture her love and respect for it when I write this story."

Photograph by Latent Image

Knowing the Words

Write the words from the story that have the meanings below.

1. in a certain neighborhood

   _____
   (Par. 1)

2. life work

   _____
   (Par. 3)

3. made-up story

   _____
   (Par. 7)

4. reasonable opinions or decisions

   _____
   (Par. 8)

5. get hold of

   _____
   (Par. 12)

6. Write **S** between each pair of words that are synonyms, words with similar meanings.

   professor ____ teacher

   career ____ occupation

   young ____ old

   rising ____ falling

   university ____ school

Learning to Study

You remember that entry words are divided into syllables. This shows where the words can be divided at the end of a line of writing. Divide the words below into syllables.

1. s c i e n t i s t
2. l i b r a r y
3. c a r e e r
4. i n t e r v i e w
5. a l w a y s
6. e x p e r i m e n t
7. f i c t i o n
8. c a p t u r e

Reading and Thinking

1. Check the main idea of the story.

   ____ the science fair

   ____ an interesting interview

   ____ famous scientists

2. Check each word on phrase below that describes Dr. Stevens.

   ____ shy

   ____ lazy

   ____ enjoys science

   ____ helpful

Put **F** before the sentences that are facts.
Put **O** before the sentences that are opinions.

3. ____ Experiments are done to test theories.

4. ____ Science is the best subject.

5. ____ People have stood on the moon.

6. Number the steps in the order they occur.

   ____ A scientist develops an idea.

   ____ Conclusions are drawn.

   ____ Results of an experiment are studied.

   ____ Experiments are done to test the idea.

Working with Words

Fill in each blank with the possessive form of the word in parentheses.

1. The _____ stars are countless. (sky)

2. The _____ book tells about the names of the stars. (astronomer)

3. The _____ ideas were tested in the lab. (scientist)

Roughing It

Read this story to learn how our wildlife can be saved.

1   On Tuesday, Uncle Max joined Tom and his family for dinner. Passing the green beans, he said, "Tom, I was wondering if you'd like to go camping in the mountains with me this weekend."

2   Tom hesitated for a moment. Then he said, "I'm not sure, Uncle Max. What did you have in mind?"

3   "Well, I have to write a story about endangered animals for the paper. That's why I thought it would be a good idea if I went up to the mountains. Let's face it, I just won't get a feel for nature if I stay in my apartment in the city."

4   "Do you mean those animals are in danger of something?" asked Meg.

5   "That's exactly what I mean," said Uncle Max. "We keep cutting down forests and building shopping centers where these animals used to live. People have to see that there's a problem, which is why my story is so important."

6   "Sure, I'll go camping with you, Uncle Max," Tom said. "Would you mind if my friend Lance came along?"

7   "That's fine with me," answered Uncle Max.

8   On Saturday morning, Uncle Max and the boys got an early start. The mountain scenery was breathtaking. Once they'd chosen a campsite, the boys looked for firewood.

9   The three campers enjoyed a light supper and sat back to relax in their peaceful surroundings. "It seems hard to believe that animals could be in danger in a place as beautiful as this," Lance said.

10   "You're right, Lance," Uncle Max remarked. "That's why my piece for the *Bulletin* is so important. In the past, uncontrolled hunting was the main cause of

animal extinction. But now, many wild animals in the United States are protected by laws. These laws limit hunting and fishing."

11   "What is endangering animals now?" Tom asked.

12   "Some of their homes are being destroyed by pollution. In other cases the land is being used for homes, farms, and highways. That leaves less room for animals to live and grow," said Uncle Max.

13   "What can be done to save them?" Lance asked.

14   "Some land has to be set aside as national parks or wildlife shelters. Game wardens have to watch out for people who are hunting out of season or fishing without a license. Although most hunters are responsible, there are still some people who have no respect for wildlife," Uncle Max sighed.

15   "I'm glad you invited us, Uncle Max," Tom said. "I just didn't know how much animals depend on us for their survival. Your story will help all of us."

Photograph by Alan Carey

Knowing the Words

Write the words from the story that have the meanings below.

1. not safe

_____
(Par. 3)

2. process of dying out

_____
(Par. 10)

3. something that makes the land, water, or air dirty

_____
(Par. 12)

4. people who guard wildlife

_____
(Par. 14)

5. Check the sentence in which *light* has the same meaning as it does in paragraph 9.

_____ The light flickered mysteriously before going completely out.

_____ The newspaper carrier delivers papers before it is light out.

_____ A light rain covered the grass.

Working with Words

Use two words from each sentence to form a compound word, and write the new word in the blank.

1. A bird that is blue is a

_____.

2. A cloth that covers a table is a

_____.

3. A shell that can be located near the sea

is a _____.

4. Wood that is used for building a fire is

_____.

Reading and Thinking

1. Check the main idea of the story.

_____ going camping

_____ protecting wildlife

_____ working as a game warden

2. Put a **C** before the phrases that tell what you might observe in a city, and put an **F** before the phrases that tell what you might observe in a forest.

_____ deer grazing

_____ traffic moving

_____ people shopping

_____ people hunting and fishing

3. Why must a game warden check to see

that all is well in the forest? _____

_____

4. Write something Tom learned while

camping with Uncle Max. _____

_____

5. Will the people who read Uncle Max's article respect wildlife more? Why or

why not? _____

_____

Learning to Study

Check the words that would appear on a dictionary page having these guide words.

babies—backward   **icing—illness**

_____ baboon   _____ imitate

_____ bachelor   _____ idol

_____ bark   _____ ideal

_____ back   _____ icecap

_____ backward   _____ ignore

33

Lights Out

In this story, Tom learns about a strange day Ms. Lopez once had working at a city newspaper.

1   It was Thursday afternoon and Tom felt miserable. He was coming down with a cold. Even worse, it was raining. He grabbed his jacket from his locker and headed for the door. Just then he heard someone call his name.

2   "Tom, I'm so glad I caught up with you before you left!" said Ms. Lopez. "Do you think you could stay and help me? I'm laying out the next edition of the paper. I've got to drop it off to be printed at the *Bulletin* tomorrow morning."

3   Caught off guard, Tom heard himself saying, "Sure. Why not?"

4   Betsy and four other students were already in the newspaper office. They were creating headlines for each article.

5   As they worked, one of the students asked, "Ms. Lopez, you worked for a city newspaper once, didn't you?"

6   "When I was still in college, I took a summer job at *The Times* in Mill Creek, my hometown."

7   "What kind of work did you do?" asked Betsy.

8   "You name it, I did it—filing, typing, running errands. I also filled in for vacationing reporters. Luckily, one of the editors took me under her wing and showed me the ropes."

9   "It must have been incredibly exciting," said Tom.

10   "I'm not sure if *exciting* is the word I'd use. *Frantic* is more like it. It was hard, fast-paced work. The place hummed twenty-four hours a day. That is, except for one day in late summer," said Ms. Lopez.

11   "What happened?" Betsy asked.

12   "Try to imagine it: lights blazing, electric typewriters clicking away, and people running every which way. All at once, there was a tremendous roar of thunder, followed by a loud crackle. Then, everything was still."

13   "You mean . . .?"

14   "I mean the electricity went out and everything came to a complete halt. The newsroom was silent, and the presses stopped rolling. It took us all a few minutes to realize what had happened."

15   "What did you do?" Betsy asked.

16   "What could we do?" Ms. Lopez laughed. "We lit candles, brought out the old manual typewriters, and waited for the presses to start rolling again. For the first time in over ninety years, the Friday edition of *The Times* didn't make it to the newsstand on time."

Knowing the Words

Write the words from the story that have the meanings below.

1. very or unbelievably

   _____
   (Par. 9)

2. making a short, snapping sound

   _____
   (Par. 12)

3. very great

   _____
   (Par. 12)

4. understand clearly

   _____
   (Par. 14)

5. done by hand

   _____
   (Par. 16)

In each row below, circle the three words that belong together.

6. rain   thunder   heat   lightning

7. city   river   town   village

8. summer   sun   beach   snow

9. college   school   study   map

10. discuss   halt   pause   stop

Learning to Study

A **pronunciation key** is a list of sound symbols and key words. They tell how to pronounce dictionary entry words. Use the pronunciation key on the inside back cover of this book to write the words that match these respellings.

1. /nüz´ pā´ pər/   _____

2. /ärt´i kəl/   _____

3. /wən(t)s/   _____

4. /hȯlt/   _____

Reading and Thinking

Write the word that best completes each sentence.

1. The _____ poured through the hole in the barn's roof.

   newspaper   rain   exactly

2. Everyone read the good news in the

   newspaper's _____.

   headline   company   editors

3. How was *The Times* different after the storm knocked out the electricity?

   _____

   _____

4. The main idea of paragraph 16 is

   ____ the effects of the thunderstorm.

   ____ preparing the paper for printing.

   ____ Ms. Lopez's job at *The Times*.

5. When Ms. Lopez worked at *The Times*,

   she lived in _____.

6. Write one phrase the author used to describe the mood or feeling in the newsroom after the power went out.

   _____

Working with Words

Fill in each blank with the possessive form of the word in parentheses.

1. The _____ noise frightened the small child. (thunder)

2. The _____ presses stopped after a flash of lightning. (newspaper)

3. When the lights went out, Linda

   discovered that the _____
   batteries were dead. (flashlight)

Deep-Sea Diving

Read this interview to decide why a deep-sea diver needs special clothes and tools.

1   Tom and Uncle Max were on their way to Florida for a weekend visit. While they were in Florida, Uncle Max was to interview Ana Ramon, a deep-sea diver. Ana lives near Tarpon Springs, Florida. She earns her living by gathering sponges from the floor of the Gulf of Mexico.

2   Max: Your job sounds like fun, Ana.

3   Ana: Oh, it is, Max! I love my work. I'm only one out of thousands of divers who have different kinds of underwater jobs.

4   Max: I thought that most divers study marine life.

5   Ana: Many divers are marine biologists, and they do study marine life. But a number of divers perform other kinds of necessary jobs. Some divers do repair work. They patch holes in sunken ships so that the ships can be raised. They also repair foundations of dams, bridges, and docks.

6   Max: That's interesting. What other types of jobs do divers have?

7   Ana: Well, some unload valuable cargo from sunken ships. At times they have brought up shipments of gold or diamonds. Once, divers even brought up a load of wheat.

8   Max: Your diving outfit looks very heavy.

9   Ana: It is heavy! And it is very expensive! A good diving suit costs thousands of dollars. It must protect as well as clothe the diver.

10   Max: How does it protect you?

11   Ana: The suit is a "rubber sandwich"— a thin layer of rubber between layers of heavy cloth. A flat piece of metal protects the diver's chest. Under the suit, the diver also wears several pairs of long underwear to keep warm because it can be quite chilly underwater.

12   Max: Are your shoes as heavy as they look?

13   Ana: Max, they weigh twenty pounds each. They make it easier for me to stand up; and the belt, which is also very heavy, helps me to stay on the bottom of the ocean.

14   Max: Your job and other divers' jobs sound challenging. This interview will be a good story for *The Kendall Bulletin* readers.

15   Ana: I hope so, Max. Don't forget to send me a copy. Enjoy the rest of your stay in Florida.

Knowing the Words

Write the words from the story that have the meanings below.

1. people who study plants and animals

   _____
   (Par. 5)

2. freight carried by a ship

   _____
   (Par. 7)

3. a thickness or fold

   _____
   (Par. 11)

4. Write **A** between each pair of words that are antonyms, words with opposite meanings.

   sea   _____   land

   sink   _____   float

   dive   _____   plunge

Match each word with its abbreviation.

5. _____ pounds   **a.** NM

6. _____ Florida   **b.** lbs.

7. _____ New Mexico **c.** FL

Learning to Study

Read this weather report. Then answer the questions below.

> *Tarpon Times Weather*
> –Partly cloudy, warm tonight
> and Friday
> –Low tonight around 60 degrees
> –High Friday in the 80s

1. Will there be heavy rainstorms during

   the night? _____

2. The lowest temperature on Thursday

   night will be about _____.

Reading and Thinking

Write the word that best completes each sentence.

1. I am interested in studying about

   _____ animals.

   marine   certainly   helmet

2. The gift was not _____.

   various   main   expensive

3. What does Ana gather from the Gulf of

   Mexico? _____

4. Check two sentences that are true.

   _____ Divers are warmly dressed.

   _____ A diver's clothes are expensive.

   _____ All divers are marine biologists.

5. The author wrote this story to

   _____ describe Tarpon Springs, Florida.

   _____ explain marine biology.

   _____ inform readers about diving.

6. Ana knows a great deal about diving

   equipment because _____

   _____

Working with Words

Rewrite each group of words below. Use possessive forms.

1. shoes of the diver _____

2. members of the team _____

3. tools of the crew _____

4. suit that belongs to Ana _____

5. cargo of the ship _____

6. floor of the ocean _____

7. story written by Max _____

37

Uncle Max's Friend

In this story, you'll discover what Uncle Max was like as a young reporter.

1   "Where have you been?" said the woman sternly. "I was beginning to think you'd forgotten our lunch date."

2   "You're as bad-tempered as ever, Agnes," laughed Uncle Max, grasping her hand. "I guess that's one reason it's so good to see you again. I was afraid you might have mellowed."

3   "Ripened, yes. Mellow, never."

4   Tom stared in astonishment at the woman sitting across from him. She didn't seem to notice him at all.

5   "Well, you're certainly as lovely as ever," continued Uncle Max.

6   "Trying to butter me up as usual. Why don't you tell the truth? Just say I was a good reporter. Lovely has nothing to do with it," she snapped. Then looking at Tom, she went on, "You've forgotten something, Max."

7   Quickly, Uncle Max introduced Tom to his friend and one-time coworker, Agnes Moore. Then, he went on to explain, "Tom went with me yesterday to interview Ana Ramon, the deep-sea diver."

8   Shaking his hand firmly, Agnes said, "How fortunate you are, Son, to be related to this very special man. What a team we made at the *Bulletin* in our time."

9   "It's a pleasure to meet you," Tom stammered. Tom wasn't quite sure what to make of this interesting woman.

10   "Why, I remember when your Uncle Max got his first assignment. There he was, a young reporter. Max was as eager as a beaver to write his first story. You certainly learned from that assignment!" Agnes exclaimed.

11   "You bet I did!" Max agreed.

12   "What happened?" Tom asked.

13   "It seems that one of Kendall's largest corporations was losing money. People on the inside thought one of the company's accountants was taking the money for himself. Your Uncle Max was told to interview the head accountant. Well, he spoke to him all right. He said the vice-president had told him she was ready to fire the suspect. Max wrote his story, but he made one mistake. He failed to check with the vice-president to see if she actually had made that comment. The story had to be pulled at the last minute. Then we had to rush around trying to find some smaller pieces to fill the space. Meanwhile, we checked all of the other facts," Agnes finished.

14   "Checking facts is something a good reporter always does," Uncle Max said. "I really learned my lesson."

Knowing the Words

Write the words from the story that have the meanings below.

1. became more gentle

_____
(Par. 2)

2. spoke with stops and starts

_____
(Par. 9)

3. really

_____
(Par. 13)

4. What is the simile in paragraph 10?

_____

_____

5. Circle the three words that belong together.

friend   enemy

acquaintance   playmate

Learning to Study

In each blank, write the name of the correct reference book.

atlas   thesaurus   almanac

1. Where could you look to find out how many miles Tarpon Springs is from

Cape Canaveral? _____

2. Where could you look to find out some

of the major events of 1997? _____

3. Where could you find a synonym for

research? _____

4. Where could you look to find the name

of the governor of Florida? _____

Reading and Thinking

Write the word that best completes each sentence.

1. Lynn was _____ to begin her art lessons.

suspicious   eager   lazy

2. Jeff _____ the reporter to his class.

introduced   laughed   rejected

3. The main idea of paragraph 13 is

____ being an accountant.

____ the importance of checking the facts.

____ working for a large corporation.

4. Max's story did not appear in the paper

because _____

_____ .

5. How did Uncle Max's reporting style change after his story was pulled from the paper?

_____

Working with Words

These nouns have base words that are verbs. Fill in the chart.

	Noun	Verb	Suffix
1.	rotation	_____	_____
2.	assignment	_____	_____
3.	adoption	_____	_____
4.	objection	_____	_____
5.	replacement	_____	_____
6.	imagination	_____	_____
7.	payment	_____	_____

A Visit from the City Editor

Read this story to learn about working at a newspaper company.

1 One day, *The Kendall Bulletin's* city editor, Jim Martinez, came to Tom's journalism class.

2 Mr. Martinez leaned back in a chair. He studied the faces of the students around him. Then he started to talk. "I'll tell you a little about what the newspaper business is like. I hope you want to know how I got into this business, since that's why I'm here."

3 The students laughed and he continued, "When I was nine or ten, I wrote a letter to the editor of our local paper. I thought that the first day of summer should be a holiday, and I said so. When I saw my name in print, I was hooked. A month later, I sent in a story I'd written about the Independence Day parade I was in. Somebody must have liked it because it was published. Better yet, I got a check in the mail! To love what you do and get paid for it, too—that's as good as it gets."

4 "What's the most important job at a paper?" asked Betsy.

5 "That's a tough one. Each job is important. But I'd say that the reporters are the paper's core. They are responsible for investigating and writing the stories. When the reporters go out to cover a story, they'll often be accompanied by a photographer. That's who must try to capture a whole story in just one picture. A story just wouldn't be the same without a photo to go with it."

6 Then Tom asked, "What's the difference between a city editor and a copy editor?"

7 "Well, as city editor, my main job is to assign each story to a reporter."

8 "What does a copy editor do?" Laura asked.

9 "After a story is typed, the copy editors read it. Carefully, they check to make sure there are no mistakes in grammar, wording, spelling, or facts. It's the same thing you do here before you hand in an article to Ms. Lopez. The copy editors make sure all the questions from the story have been answered. As a last step, they type in a headline. Then the story is ready to be printed."

10 "Then what about the managing editor?" Betsy asked.

11 "Well, among other things, the managing editor helps to decide what stories to run and approves what we call a dummy sheet. Sometimes I help with the dummy sheet."

12 "What's a dummy sheet?" asked several students at once.

13 "It's like a map. We have to decide where each item goes and how much space to give it. We plot it all on sheets of paper, just like these."

14 He passed around the sample dummy sheets. Mr. Martinez ended by saying, "When you visit the paper on Thursday, I'll show you how it all fits together."

Knowing the Words

Write the words from the story that have the meanings below.

1. appeared in print

_____
(Par. 3)

2. central part

_____
(Par. 5)

3. give out

_____
(Par. 7)

4. accepts or gives permission for

_____
(Par. 11)

Circle the word with the correct meaning in each sentence below.

5. I (know, no) where the bank is located.

6. We brought (our, hour) lunches with us when we attended the concert.

7. The girls placed (they're, their) shoes in the trunk.

8. What are you going to (where, wear) to the festival?

Working with Words

The suffixes **-hood** and **-ship** usually mean "the state or condition of being." Add **-hood** and **-ship** to each word below. Then use the new word in a sentence.

1. child _____

_____

2. leader _____

_____

3. neighbor _____

_____

Reading and Thinking

1. Number the events in the order in which they happen.

_____ The dummy sheet is approved by the managing editor.

_____ The city editor assigns each story to a reporter.

_____ The copy editor types a headline for the story.

_____ The copy editor checks the facts in the story.

_____ The reporter investigates and writes the story.

Put **F** before the sentences that are facts. Put **O** before the sentences that are opinions.

2. _____ The reporters have the most important job at the paper.

3. _____ A city editor gives each story to a reporter.

4. _____ The copy editor's job is the hardest.

5. _____ The dummy sheets show where each item in the paper will go.

6. _____ A photographer often accompanies the reporter.

7. The author wrote this story to

_____ invite people to a newspaper firm.

_____ tell about the newspaper business.

_____ describe Jim Martinez's job.

Learning to Study

Check the reference source you might use to find out more about newspaper publishing.

_____ an atlas

_____ an encyclopedia

_____ a dictionary

_____ a thesaurus

The Kendall Bulletin

Read this story to learn important facts about publishing a newspaper.

1 On Thursday, Mr. Martinez took Tom and the rest of the class to the newsroom of the *Bulletin.* It was a long, bright room filled with rows of desks. Each desk had its own computer. "Those reporters, you see, are typing in their stories," Mr. Martinez said.

2 He went on, "Once a story is typed into the computer, the copy editor edits it. Then the story's headline is typed. As the last step, a code is entered."

3 "What does that do?" Betsy asked.

4 "It tells the computer to send the story upstairs. That's where the typesetting machine is. Follow me and I'll show you."

5 Mr. Martinez led the students to the composing room. Walking them over to the typesetting machine, he continued, "The computer feeds the story to this machine. It comes out on a roll of film, which is then developed. Next, as you can see, the stories come out here on narrow sheets. The sheets show us how the stories will appear in the paper.

6 "The sheets are then brought over here," he explained. He led them to rows of slanted tabletops. "A member of the make-up crew runs each sheet through one of these waxing machines. That way, it will stick to the layout sheet, but can be lifted off and moved if necessary. Then the stories are placed on the layout sheets, page by page."

7 Tom excitedly nudged Betsy, "Wait until you see this!"

8 Before she could reply, Mr. Martinez led them to what seemed to be the largest camera in the world. "Fran will tell you what happens next."

9 "I take these completed layout sheets and feed them into this camera," Fran said. "As you see here, a negative comes out." With that, Fran held up a large plastic sheet. "The printing on the negative, of course, is backward. I then send the negative in one of these tubes to the press room."

10 Thanking her, the class left the composing room. They went with Mr. Martinez to the room where the press operators worked. Here, each negative got a thin coat of acid. This process burned the print and pictures from the negative onto a large orange, waxy-looking sheet. Each sheet would then be set onto the press. There, the next edition of *The Kendall Bulletin* would be printed. Once it was folded and cut, it would be ready for delivery.

11 Tom and his classmates followed Mr. Martinez back to the newsroom. As he thanked Mr. Martinez, Tom said, "The more I know about this business, the more I am sure that it's the business for me."

Photograph by Ted Rice

Knowing the Words

Write the words from the story that have the meanings below.

1. setting the words into type

   _____
   (Par. 4)

2. setting up type

   _____
   (Par. 5)

3. pushed lightly

   _____
   (Par. 7)

4. Check the sentence in which *sheet* has the same meaning as it does in paragraph 5.

   _____ Barb put a clean sheet on the bed.

   _____ Ms. Lopez handed me the answer sheet after I sharpened my pencil.

   _____ Meg washed the cookie sheet after she finished baking.

Learning to Study

Look at the time line and answer the questions below.

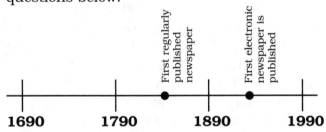

1. How many years does the line between each pair of dates stand for? _____

2. Which of the two events on the time line occurred first? _____

   _____

3. Would the year 2090 be on the right or left side of the time line? _____

Reading and Thinking

Write the word that best completes each sentence.

1. The headline was _____ into the computer.

   written   typed   addressed

2. Mr. Martinez _____ the students into the composing room.

   refused   run   led

3. Who writes the story's headline?

   _____

4. Who prepares the layout sheet?

   _____

5. Why did Tom think Betsy would be excited to see the *Bulletin's* camera?

   _____

6. Do you think Tom will work at the *Bulletin* someday? Give reasons for your answer.

   _____

   _____

Working with Words

Use two words from each sentence to form a compound word, and write the compound word in the blank.

1. A coat worn in the rain is a _____.

2. A tie that is worn around the neck is a

   _____.

3. A brush that is used for cleaning each

   tooth is a _____.

4. A ball that is thrown through a basket

   is a _____.

43

Thanks to the Computer

As you read, you'll discover how newspaper printing has changed over the years.

1 Tom returned to *The Kendall Bulletin* Monday after school. He was doing an article for the school paper about *The Kendall Bulletin's* one hundredth anniversary. He needed some material. Uncle Max had offered to help him.

2 Tom pulled up a chair. He then told his uncle what he had in mind. "I'll write a short history of the paper, of course. But I really want to focus on some of the changes that have taken place through the years."

3 "Well, you've come to the right person," Uncle Max laughed. "I've been around a long time!"

4 Uncle Max pointed to the video display terminal in his office. "The VDT has made a big difference in how we do things around here. A copy editor can check and correct the story quickly," Uncle Max said. "This type of computer has helped editors and reporters save a great deal of time and paper."

5 "Things must run a lot faster nowadays," Tom said.

6 "I'll say," Uncle Max replied. "Let's go down to the basement, and I'll show you something."

7 Tom soon found himself in a dusty room. It was filled with outdated equipment.

8 "This is a Linotype machine," Uncle Max said.

9 Staring down at it, Tom said, "This part with the keys looks just like a typewriter."

10 "Yes, it does. The Linotype operator would sit down in front of that keyboard and type in each line of a story, letter by letter. When the line was completed, the operator would press a key to set the line. Lead inside the machine would heat up and fill the letter molds. As the lead cooled, it would harden into a line of type with raised letters. The blocks of letters would be fitted together in one of those wooden frames on that table over there. Then they were coated with ink. The newspaper was slowly printed, page by page. The *Bulletin* used to have thirty of these machines going at once. Thanks to computers, printing the paper doesn't take nearly as long as it used to."

11 "Are Linotype machines used at all these days?" Tom asked.

12 "Not much in the United States," Uncle Max said. "However, Linotypes are still used in many parts of Africa and South America."

13 "Thanks for your help, Uncle Max," Tom said. "I think my readers will like my story about how the *Bulletin* is printed."

Knowing the Words

Write the words from the story that have the meanings below.

1. yearly celebration

_____
(Par. 1)

2. old-fashioned

_____
(Par. 7)

Find a synonym (word with similar meaning) in the story for each of these words.

3. story _____
(Par. 1)

4. concentrate _____
(Par. 2)

5. quicker _____
(Par. 5)

6. cellar _____
(Par. 6)

7. assistance _____
(Par. 13)

Learning to Study

Read the dictionary entries and answer the questions below.

^{1}**type** /tīp/ *n* **1** a class or group having common characteristics **2** printed or typewritten letters

^{2}**type** *v* to write with a typewriter

1. In which entry is *type* a noun?

_____

2. In which entry is *type* a verb?

_____

3. How many syllables does *type* have? ___

4. Look at entry ^{1}**type**. Which definition gives the meaning of *type* as it is used

in paragraph 4? ___

Reading and Thinking

1. Number the events in the order in which they happen.

____ The Linotype operator types each line.

____ The lead blocks are coated with ink.

____ The newspaper is printed page by page.

____ The lead inside the Linotype machine heats up.

____ The blocks of letters are fitted together.

2. Write one way the *Bulletin* newsroom is different now than when the newspaper

was first founded. _____

_____

Write the word that best completes each sentence.

3. Air _____ can be a problem in a large city.

deadlines   keyboards   pollution

4. Meg spoke _____ about the new bike.

furiously   excitedly   friendly

Working with Words

Rewrite each group of words below. Use possessive forms.

1. the wings of the birds

_____

2. the tail of the monkey

_____

3. the game that belongs to Kim

_____

Runners, to Your Marks

Have you ever forgotten something really important? Read this story to see what Tom forgot.

1   Stopping by Tom's locker, Lance reminded him. "Don't forget track practice today."

2   "It's a good thing you came by, Lance," Tom said, "I knew there was something I was supposed to do today. I just couldn't remember what!"

3   After school, Tom changed into his sweat suit and running shoes. Then he and Lance met their teammates by the outdoor track where they started warming up.

4   Clapping his hands forcefully, Coach Palmer signaled the boys to come to attention. "We've been over this before, but it's worth repeating. We lost our meet against Morristown High because we made some careless mistakes. Now we face Kingston. I want you fellows to look good and run them into the ground!"

5   With that, everyone yelled enthusiastically.

6   "You haven't won yet," Coach Palmer reminded them. "Our conditioning is right where it should be. Now let's remember how important technique is. Finish limbering up and then we'll see what you can do."

7   After warming up, Tom approached the starting line. "Runners, to your marks," called the starter. Preparing for his one-hundred-meter run, Tom crouched into position in the starting blocks. He tucked his left foot behind him and knelt on the track.

8   At the words *get set,* Tom raised himself up and waited for the *go* command. Hearing that, he broke away and raced down the track.

9   "Do it again, Ellis!" shouted the coach as Tom finished his first one-hundred-meter run. "This time, remember to keep low and watch your form," Coach Palmer added.

10   As he was nearing the end of his second run, Tom suddenly remembered something that hit him like a ton of bricks. "I'm supposed to be interviewing the mayor right now!" Tom exclaimed.

11   Without breaking his stride, Tom dashed for the locker room, grabbed his gear, and raced frantically out to the car.

12   "Hey, Tom," Lance shouted after him. "Wait up. Where are you going in such a hurry?"

13   Tom turned from the parking lot and said, "I completely forgot my interview with the mayor. If I hurry, I might still make it." With that, Tom got into the car. Lowering the window, he added, "Tell Coach Palmer I'll make up the time tomorrow."

14   "I'll take care of it," Lance assured him. "Good luck."

15   Tom pulled out of the school parking lot, still wondering how he'd ever explain his tardiness to the mayor.

Knowing the Words

Write the words from the story that have the meanings below.

1. with strength

_____
(Par. 4)

2. method

_____
(Par. 6)

3. warming up

_____
(Par. 6)

4. What is the simile in paragraph 10?

_____

_____

Working with Words

The prefix **un-** means "not" or "the opposite of." For example, the word *unlock* means "the opposite of lock," while the word *unsafe* means "not safe." Add **un-** to each of the words, and write the new words in the blanks.

happy   tie

1. Denise began to _____ the twisted knot in her shoestring.

2. The small child looked _____ as she watched the balloon float away.

The prefix **dis-** can also mean "not" or "the opposite of." Write words that have the following meanings by adding the prefix **dis-** to a base word. Then use the new word in a sentence.

3. not like _____

_____

4. the opposite of connect _____

_____

Reading and Thinking

1. Check the main idea of the story.

____ running on the track team

____ a forgotten meeting

____ becoming a track star

2. Tom will be late for his interview with

the mayor because _____

_____.

3. How do you think the mayor will react once Tom arrives for the interview?

_____

_____

4. Describe the kind of person Coach

Palmer is. _____

Learning to Study

This is part of an application. It is the paper that students must fill out when they want to join the track team. Read the application and answer the questions.

```
NAME _____
        Last        First        Middle
ADDRESS _____
        Number              Street
        _____
        City        State        ZIP
BIRTH DATE _____
        Day         Month        Year
```

1. What part of the name is written last?

_____

2. What part of the application tells the

person's age? _____

3. What should be written first on the

address line? _____

Better Late Than Never

Did Tom interview the mayor? Read this story and find out.

1   Tom was filled with anxiety as he headed down Broad Street. How could he have forgotten such an important interview? Ms. Lopez was counting on him to produce another front-page story. He had to make it on time, but rush hour had already started. Hundreds of drivers were headed home after a long day of work.

2   Tom's interview with the mayor had been set for four o'clock. It was almost five o'clock when he finally found a parking spot. Slamming the door, he sprinted down the street and raced up the steps of City Hall. Entering the building, he made his way to the mayor's office.

3   Leaning on a desk, he all but shouted at the secretary. "Where's the mayor? I've got to see him right away!"

4   Coolly, the finely dressed gentleman behind the desk looked up and asked, "And just who are you?"

5   "I'm Tom Ellis, sir," he blurted.

6   The man said nothing, and simply stared at Tom. Awkwardly, Tom looked down at himself and groaned. He was standing in the mayor's office in City Hall wearing the sweaty clothes he'd worn at track practice. His hair was all tangled, and he knew his face was flushed from running.

7   "I can explain, sir," Tom began, "if you'll only listen. I had an appointment to interview the mayor at four o'clock," he stammered. "I'm doing a story about him for *The Knightly News* and . . ."

8   Tom was cut off by the wave of a hand. "The mayor left fifteen minutes ago. He's giving a speech tonight and couldn't be late."

9   "Of course not," Tom answered quietly, sinking into a nearby chair. What could he do now? He needed a story for the front page of the paper. What was he going to tell

Ms. Lopez? This wasn't the first time his forgetfulness had let someone down. His mother had been the victim of his poor memory on many occasions.

10   Tom headed for home, lost in thought over the story that was due the next morning. As he pulled into the driveway of his home, an idea came to him. He entered the house and went up to his room. Tom sat down at his desk and began his article by typing the title, "Losing My Head." Maybe through this story he could explore the many things that could happen when people forget. He'd start with himself and go all the way to the President of the United States. The story might not be as good as an interview with the mayor. But it could be a good way to show the readers some of the funny and not so funny things that happen when people forget.

Knowing the Words

Write the words from the story that have the meanings below.

1. ran at full speed

_____
(Par. 2)

2. became red suddenly

_____
(Par. 6)

3. person who is treated badly

_____
(Par. 9)

Circle the word with the correct meaning in each sentence below.

4. Because the crowd was in her (way, weigh), Beth couldn't cross the street.

5. Do you know (wear, where) my running shoes are?

6. Please (pour, poor) the water into the bigger glass.

Find a synonym (word with similar meaning) in the story for each of these words.

7. worry _____
(Par. 1)

8. article _____
(Par. 7)

Learning to Study

Use the pronunciation key on the inside back cover of this book to write the words that match these respellings.

1. /vik´ təm/ _____

2. /ang zī´ ət ē/ _____

3. /òf´ ə s/ _____

4. /fīn´ əl ē/ _____

5. /mā´ ər/ _____

Reading and Thinking

Write the word that best completes each sentence.

1. Jenny _____ the door as she hurried to catch the bus.

slammed   poked   started

2. The tall _____ is at the corner of First and Third Streets.

mayor   building   desk

3. The mayor's _____ was heard by hundreds of citizens.

office   speech   raincoat

4. What time was Tom's appointment to interview the mayor? _____

5. What did Tom decide to write his article about? _____

6. Tom wasn't able to interview the mayor because _____.

7. Do you think Tom will remember important appointments from now on?

Give reasons for your answer. _____

_____

Working with Words

Use a word from row A and a word from row B to form a compound word to complete each sentence. The word you form must make sense in the sentence.

A. book   bed   any
B. one   case   room

1. Has _____ seen my notebook?

2. I think I left it in my _____.

3. Please look on the top shelf of my

_____.

Handtalk

Read this story to learn about American Sign Language.

1 "I'm glad you decided to visit us, Tom. You'll learn much more than you would have by interviewing me on the phone," said Dr. Hayman, head of the Beam School for the Deaf.

2 "Thank you for inviting me. I'll be honest. I know very little about sign language and lip reading," Tom said.

3 "Sign language is a language of gestures and hand symbols," said Dr. Hayman. "Many people in the United States who are hearing impaired use American Sign Language."

4 "Is it true that American Sign Language was not accepted as a true language until the 1960s?" Tom asked.

5 "Yes. Many teachers and parents would not use it. Now, though, it's one of the main ways of training hearing impaired people to communicate. Ameslan, a shorter word for American Sign Language, is based on ideas rather than words. The shape of the hand and its position next to the body express certain ideas."

6 "Dr. Hayman, I read that sixty percent of Ameslan is based on the French system," Tom said.

7 "That's true," she said. "You see, our very first teacher of hearing impaired people was French. Laurent Clerc, a deaf person, taught French Sign Language in Paris. He came here in the early 1800s. Naturally, he brought sign language with him. Would you like to visit with some of our students?"

8 "I certainly would," said Tom.

9 As Tom and Dr. Hayman entered the classroom, they were greeted by the throbbing sounds of a popular song. Singing the words, the students clapped their hands and danced.

10 "How can they do that?" Tom asked.

11 "They're getting the beat from the vibrations of the music," Dr. Hayman explained. "They can feel the vibrations through their feet."

12 When the song ended, Tom clapped appreciatively. Then the students drew him farther into the room. Several raised their right hands to their temples as if saluting. They were signing the word *hello.*

13 "Why don't you introduce yourself?" Dr. Hayman suggested.

14 Tom imitated the students' gesture. Letting them see his lips moving, Tom said, "My name is Tom."

15 In answer, the students' fingers moved rapidly. "They're fingerspelling their names for you," Dr. Hayman explained.

16 When it was time to go, Dr. Hayman said, "Why don't I show you how to thank them? Just place your hand on your mouth. Now, keeping your elbow against your body, swing your forearm downward."

17 In return, the students first bent the fingers of their right hands. Then, keeping their palms facing forward, they moved their hands up and down, and signed the word *goodbye.*

Knowing the Words

Write the words from the story that have the meanings below.

1. motions used to express ideas

_____
(Par. 3)

2. not able to hear fully

_____
(Par. 3)

3. express ideas and thoughts

_____
(Par. 5)

4. using gestures to speak

_____
(Par. 12)

5. Check the sentence in which *drew* has the same meaning as it does in paragraph 12.

_____ Sharon drew a beautiful picture of daffodils.

_____ We drew nearer to the warmth of the campfire.

_____ He drew the wrong conclusion from the facts that were presented.

Working with Words

The prefix **fore-** means "front" or "before." For example, the word *forearm* means "the front of the arm." Add **fore-** to each word. Then use the new word in a sentence.

1. head _____

_____

2. cast _____

_____

3. told _____

_____

Reading and Thinking

1. *Ameslan* is another word for

_____ .

2. Where did Laurent Clerc teach French Sign Language? _____

3. Why did Dr. Hayman tell Tom he would learn more from a personal interview?

_____

_____

4. The author wrote this story to

_____ invite readers to visit the Beam School.

_____ explain hearing impairments.

_____ inform readers about American Sign Language.

5. Write a fact Tom learned about American Sign Language.

_____

6. Write an opinion that Tom may have formed after his trip to the Beam School

for the Deaf. _____

_____

Learning to Study

Complete this outline.

I. The History of American Sign Language

A. _____

B. _____

II. Using American Sign Language

A. _____

B. _____

The Antique Show

In this story, you'll discover what makes something an antique.

1 Tom and Meg scrambled into the back seat of their uncle's car. Tom said to Uncle Max, "Thanks for lending me your old white buck shoes. Our Fifties Day at school was a fantastic success this year!"

2 "Those were the days," Uncle Max sighed.

3 "Since we're talking about the good old days, I suppose it's fitting that we're going to an antique show," Tom remarked.

4 "Now, don't be so hard on the word *old*," Uncle Max scolded good-naturedly. "Besides, a show like this comes to town only once a year."

5 "You really like antiques, don't you, Uncle Max?" Meg asked.

6 "Let me put it this way, Meggie. When the best dealers around show their wares like this, I want to be there. With the way I feel about antiques, covering the show for the paper is a bonus!"

7 "How old does an item have to be before it's considered an antique?" Meg asked.

8 "Sometimes, I feel like one myself," Uncle Max laughed, "but actually, I'd first have to be at least one hundred years old."

9 "Do you mean that just because something is one hundred years old, it is an antique?" Meg asked uncertainly.

10 "Not at all, Meg. The item also has to have a certain charm to it. Now, that doesn't necessarily mean it has to be really fancy. It can be a very simple piece, or it can be a piece that brings to mind a past way of life. In fact, it can be something as ordinary as a glass pitcher."

11 The three of them wandered about the show for several hours looking at antiques. Uncle Max hurriedly took notes for his story. He also tried to answer Meg's and Tom's questions.

12 "Ooh, look at this!" cried Meg, pointing to a mirror. It stood only fifteen inches tall with a colored glass frame. "This card says it was made in China around the year 1800."

13 "I like this wing chair," said Tom.

14 "Those wings you see sticking out of the sides were designed to protect a person from drafts. When that chair was first used, there was no such thing as central heating," Uncle Max explained.

15 As Uncle Max spoke, he spotted a small shelf clock set in a beautifully decorated wooden frame. The card resting at its base read "Walnut kitchen piece—1860."

16 "I've got to have it!" Uncle Max exclaimed. "It will look great on the mantel above my fireplace." With that, he put away his paper and pencil and took out his wallet.

Knowing the Words

Write the words from the story that have the meanings below.

1. very old furniture and accessories

   _____
   (Par. 3)

2. people who buy and sell

   _____
   (Par. 6)

3. items for sale

   _____
   (Par. 6)

4. something extra

   _____
   (Par. 6)

In each row below, circle the three words that belong together.

5. couch   chair   grass   table

6. dealer   story   merchant   wares

7. China   Florida   Japan   Asia

8. walnut   oak   pine   sand

Circle the word with the correct meaning in each sentence below.

9. Shopping for antiques is (your, you're) favorite way to relax.

10. Did you (buy, by) any antiques today?

Working with Words

Fill in each blank with the possessive form of the word in parenthesis.

1. The _____ wares were on display. (dealers)

2. The _____ prices were marked on small cards. (antiques)

3. _____ notes were left on the table. (Diane)

Reading and Thinking

Write the word that best completes each sentence.

1. Antique collecting is a _____ hobby.

   level   broken   popular

2. The _____ is planning a furniture sale.

   merchant   lumber   portrait

3. How old must an item be before it is

   considered an antique? _____

4. What was the purpose of a wing chair?

   _____

   _____

Put **F** before the sentences that are facts. Put **O** before the sentences that are opinions.

5. _____ Everyone likes collecting antiques.

6. _____ The best antiques are found in small antique shops.

7. _____ If an item is old enough and charming enough, it can become an antique.

8. _____ Some people collect antique cars.

Learning to Study

Read the dictionary entry below. Then answer the questions.

wing / wing / n **1** one of the movable parts of a bird or insect used in flying **2** part that sticks out from the main part or body

1. What part of speech is *wing*? _____

2. Which definition gives the meaning of

   wing as it is used in paragraph 13? _____

53

A Taste of China

In this story, you'll learn about life in China.

1   It was Sunday, and Betsy and some of her friends were gathered at the park. Kwan Lee, an exchange student, had arrived earlier that week from China. She would be living with Betsy's family while she studied at Kendall High School.

2   "There's so much to ask you, Kwan," Betsy said. "I hope you don't mind. It's just that I can't imagine going to a foreign country to study. I mean, what's it like to have all your books printed in English?"

3   "I have studied English since I was a little girl," said Kwan, "so the books I will use will not seem so strange. Still, it will take me a while to get used to listening to English. You see, in Chinese, the tone used in saying a word can alter its meaning."

4   "Tell us a little about your country," Susan said.

5   "I come from the port city of Jiangmen in southern China on the Si River. On my way to school, I like to watch the boats. The river people stop at our town for several days to reload. Then a school teacher, like my mother, goes on board to tutor the children. All our teachers are paid by the government. My father is a doctor and he, too, is paid by the government. He does not charge his patients as doctors do here."

6   "Does he really use pins and operate while people are awake?" Betsy asked.

7   "That's correct. My father inserts a small needle in a certain nerve center so that he can operate while the patient is conscious. Many patients go back to work the same day," she said, smiling.

8   Later, as Betsy and Kwan headed toward the Davis home, Kwan said, "The pace of life here seems much faster than it is in China."

9   "What do you mean?" Betsy asked.

10   "In my country, every afternoon we have a rest period. Even the shops close. Some people play checkers, while others often go to the movies. Then at the end of the day, everyone goes home for dinner. My father often entertains us by playing the *pi pa*. It is much like a fiddle," said Kwan as she and Betsy entered the Davis kitchen. Kwan lifted a wok to the counter.

11   "How do you use that?" asked Betsy curiously.

12   "A wok is similar to a frying pan. It gets so hot, the food cooks in just a few minutes," explained Kwan.

13   "First, we'll heat a little oil, and then add this sliced chicken. We'll heat the chicken for just a minute or two. After removing the chicken, we'll quickly stir-fry the vegetables in the oil."

14   "What's next?"

15   "Just heat everything together for a minute, serve it with some rice and then dig in—with chopsticks, of course!"

Knowing the Words

Write the words from the story that have the meanings below.

1. sound

_____
(Par. 3)

2. teach

_____
(Par. 5)

3. puts in

_____
(Par. 7)

Find an antonym (word that has opposite meaning) in the story for each of these words.

4. departed _____
(Par. 1)

5. seldom _____
(Par. 10)

Learning to Study

Look at the map and answer the questions below.

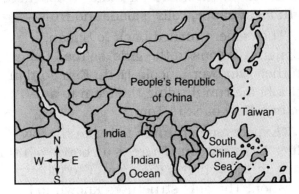

1. Which island country is southeast of China? _____

2. Which body of water is southwest of Taiwan? _____

3. Which body of water is south of India? _____

Reading and Thinking

1. What is the name of the port city that Kwan Lee comes from? _____

2. What jobs do Kwan's father and mother have? _____

3. From the story, write one way that China and the United States are alike.

_____

_____

4. From the story, write one way that China and the United States are different.

_____

_____

5. Summarize the important information of paragraph 10 in one sentence.

_____

_____

6. The author wrote this story to

_____ explain how to cook in a wok.

_____ talk about traveling.

_____ describe life in China.

Working with Words

The suffix **-ment** often means "the state or condition of being." For example, the word *retirement* means "the state or condition of being retired." Write a word to match each definition below. Then write a sentence using each word.

1. the state of being improved _____

_____

2. the state of being excited _____

_____

The News Journal

In this story, Tom and his classmates try a new way of reporting the news.

1   "OK, Tom, you've got about ten minutes before air time. Try to relax," advised Ms. Lopez.

2   "Relax! Are you kidding? I haven't been able to do that since you suggested we try this."

3   "You still like the idea of a televised news journal, don't you?" Ms. Lopez asked.

4   "Of course I do, or I wouldn't have tried out to be an announcer," Tom answered.

5   "Well, then, what's the problem?"

6   "I can answer that," said Susan, another announcer. "We're just nervous about being seen on television by the whole school."

7   "You'll both do great," urged Lance.

8   Then the overhead lights snapped on, covering the studio in bright light, and Lance called, "Take your places."

9   "Five, four, three, two, one," prompted Ms. Lopez, talking into the microphone attached to her headphone.

10   Right on signal, Betsy aimed her camera at Tom.

11   "Good morning and welcome to the first edition of *The Kendall High News Journal.* Today is Monday, March thirtieth."

12   "Five, four, three, two, one," said Ms. Lopez again.

13   Now it was Susan's turn. "At the top of the news, we'd like to welcome Kwan Lee, an exchange student from China. Kwan Lee arrived in Kendall last week. She'll be living here until June.

14   "Now here is the question for the day. What are the only known structures that are visible from space? If you think you have the answer to today's question, give it to your teacher before the end of this broadcast. Each student with the correct answer will win a free ticket to the Third Street Theater. We'll tell you the answer at

the end of today's broadcast."

15   Tom took over again. "And now for this morning's announcements. From the music department comes word that there will be a dress rehearsal for tonight's concert during eighth period. Next, Dr. Malin must cancel today's meeting of the Young Astronauts Club. The lunch menu for today is spaghetti with meat sauce, rolls, salad, and fruit."

16   The camera turned back to Susan. "Congratulations to the girls' softball team on their win over Lincoln High. Kim Jordan hit a home run, leading the team to a 3–0 victory. Now back to Tom."

17   "Expect temperatures to reach the low fifties by afternoon. There is a chance of rain later on. Now, here's the answer to today's question. The only structures known to be visible from space are the Great Wall of China and Japan's new Kansai International Airport."

18   Susan finished by saying, "From the Kendall News Team, have a great day. Your announcers for tomorrow will be Lance Deerfield and Alicia Keys."

19   Right on signal, Betsy turned her camera off as Tom let out a sigh of relief.

Knowing the Words

Write the words from the story that have the meanings below.

1. television broadcast room

_____
(Par. 8)

2. things built by human hands

_____
(Par. 14)

3. stop or do away with

_____
(Par. 15)

Find a synonym (word with similar meaning) in the story for each of these words.

4. broadcaster _____
(Par. 4)

5. positions _____
(Par. 8)

6. concluded _____
(Par. 18)

7. Check the three words that belong together.

_____ newscast _____ announcer

_____ television _____ apartment

Working with Words

The suffix **-ful** usually means "full of." For example, the word *helpful* means "full of help." Write a word to match each definition below. Then write a sentence using each word.

1. full of wonder _____

_____

2. full of cheer _____

_____

3. full of care _____

_____

Reading and Thinking

1. Number the events to show the order in which they happened.

_____ Tom announces the weather.

_____ Ms. Lopez suggested a televised news journal.

_____ Susan tells Ms. Lopez that she's nervous about doing the show.

_____ Tom tells the day's menu.

_____ Betsy aims her camera.

2. Check the words that describe Tom at the beginning of the story.

_____ nervous _____ happy

_____ relaxed _____ anxious

3. Tom tried out to be an announcer

because _____

_____.

Learning to Study

Write the name of the reference source that would provide the information needed.

dictionary   *Biographical Dictionary*
thesaurus   encyclopedia

1. Where could Julie look to find out when news reporter Walter Cronkite was born?

_____

2. Where could Tim look to find a synonym for the word *broadcast?* _____

3. Where could you look to find an article about sportscasting? _____

4. Where could Rita look to find the meaning of the word *studio?* _____

A Bag Garden

Read this story and learn about Tom's green thumb.

1   "So, tell me, Tom, how did you like covering the Flower Show?" Mrs. Ellis asked.

2   "Ma, it was wild! Every flower imaginable was in bloom," Tom said. "If you hadn't known better, you'd have thought you were outdoors. Here are some tulips and violets I bought for you. And Meg, look what I've got for you!" Tom exclaimed.

3   "A plastic bag?" Meg asked uncertainly.

4   "Now, wait a minute. I know you've wanted a vegetable garden, but you couldn't find any room for it in the backyard. Well, I've finally discovered a solution. I bought midget varieties of some of your favorites: beans, cucumbers, and tomatoes."

5   "I don't understand," Meg said.

6   "If you've got ten minutes, I'll show you," Tom replied. "Anyway, I'd like to try a bag garden before I write about it in my story."

7   "What do we do?" Meg asked.

8   "We'll begin inside so the frost can't harm the seeds. Here, take these little pots and let them soak for a while in lukewarm water."

9   "Gee, look how big they're growing!" Meg exclaimed. "What do we do with them now?"

10   "With the tip of a pencil, poke a small hole in the top of each pot and drop in a couple of seeds," Tom continued. "OK, Meg, now cover them lightly with some soil from the pot itself."

11   "Then what?" Meg asked with interest.

12   "Arrange the pots on a tray and sprinkle them with water. Now cover the tray with a sheet of plastic wrap and put the tray in a sunny window. As soon as the sprouts begin to appear, we'll remove the plastic wrap. Then when all danger of frost has passed, we'll make our bag garden."

13   "How will we do that?" Meg asked.

14   "When the time comes, we'll mix some of this plant soil with a little fertilizer and fill this bag with the mixture. Next, we'll poke a few holes in the sides of the bag, but not the bottom, so the water can drain well."

15   "What we'll probably do next," Meg suggested, "is make a little hole and plant our seedlings."

16   "That's right, the pot and everything will go right into the bag. Then we'll put the bag in a sunny spot on the porch. As the plants get bigger, we'll insert a stake in the side of the bag and tie the plants to the stake," Tom finished.

17   "Tom, this looks like a great idea," Mrs. Ellis said with satisfaction. "Meg and I will both enjoy this garden."

18   "Yes, thanks to you, Tom, this summer I can pick a salad!" Meg exclaimed.

19   "That's right," Tom agreed. "We should have enough vegetables to last through the summer. There's nothing like homegrown food!"

Knowing the Words

Write the words from the story that have the meanings below.

1. chemically made material that can be shaped

   _____
   (Par. 3)

2. unusually small

   _____
   (Par. 4)

3. different kinds

   _____
   (Par. 4)

Learning to Study

A circle graph is a chart that shows how something is divided into its different parts. This circle graph shows the percentage sold of four popular flowers that Tom saw at the Flower Show. Read the circle graph. Answer the questions below it.

1. Which flower was the most popular?

   _____

2. Which flower was least popular? _____

3. Which flower had thirty-five percent of

   the total sales? _____

4. Which flower was third in popularity?

   _____

Reading and Thinking

Write the word that best completes each sentence.

1. Jan used all her _____ planting her vegetable garden.

   appreciation   panic   energy

2. The plastic sheet offered _____ for the newly planted seeds.

   shelter   funnel   humid

3. Check the main idea of the story.

   ____ a flower show

   ____ growing African violets

   ____ planting a bag garden

4. Why didn't Tom want to plant the

   seeds outside? _____

   _____

5. Do you think Meg's bag garden will

   grow? Why or why not? _____

   _____

Working with Words

You remember that the prefix **pre-** means "before." Add **pre-** to each word and write the meaning of the word.

1. pay _____

   _____

2. view _____

   _____

3. historic _____

   _____

4. heat _____

   _____

59

The Eclipse

Read this story to learn more about eclipses of the sun and moon.

1   It was just about 12:15 A.M. when the Kendall High astronomy club arrived at the park. Tom glanced at his watch. "I still don't feel I know enough to write a story about this. Say, Dr. Malin, can you fill me in a bit on what's about to happen?"

2   "I'll be glad to," said Dr. Malin, Kendall High's astronomy teacher. "You see, just as the earth orbits the sun, the moon travels around the earth. The moon's trip takes about a month. Sometimes the earth comes between the sun and the moon. Then a lunar eclipse occurs."

3   "How often does this happen?" Betsy asked.

4   "It usually happens two or three times a year. In some years, though, it doesn't occur at all. Lunar eclipses occur less often than solar eclipses."

5   "But solar eclipses are almost never seen," Tom commented.

6   "That's because in a solar eclipse, the moon comes between the earth and the sun. Its shadow is so small, you have to be at just the right place to see it. On the other hand, eclipses of the moon can be seen by the entire half of the world that's experiencing nighttime."

7   As they talked, the eastern edge of the moon glided into the half-shadow cast by the earth. The moon was hard to see.

8   About forty minutes later, someone said, "Look! The moon has changed color."

9   "It's now making contact with the darker shadow of the earth. For the next hour, a dark coppery coating will move westward across the face of the moon."

10   Finally, the whole moon was within the shadow of the earth. Several students made sketches while Betsy took photographs for the school paper.

11   "I thought the moon would disappear since this is a total eclipse. Instead, it has a reddish glow," Tom said.

12   "The earth is blocking most of the sun's light. However, some reddish hues can curve through the earth's atmosphere to strike the moon," Dr. Malin explained. "How much depends on the amount of dust and bits of matter in the air. Volcanoes, for example, can be the cause of quite a bit of dust. Had the air been clearer, the moon would have looked brighter than this."

13   Dr. Malin and her students gathered their gear together.

14   "I can hardly wait to develop my film," Betsy said. "I hope I got some good shots."

15   "I'm sure you did," Tom said. "I took lots of notes, so I'll be able to begin writing my story tomorrow. I think Ms. Lopez will be pleased with our story about the eclipse."

Knowing the Words

Write the words from the story that have the meanings below.

1. of the moon

   _____
   (Par. 2)

2. darkness of the sun or moon

   _____
   (Par. 2)

3. of the sun

   _____
   (Par. 4)

4. shades of color

   _____
   (Par. 12)

Learning to Study

This chart shows the countries where some total solar eclipses were seen or will be seen. Read the chart and answer the questions.

	Seen from Eastern Hemisphere	Seen from Western Hemisphere
March 18, 1988	Borneo, Philippines	
July 22, 1990	Finland	
Oct. 24, 1995	Iran	
Feb. 26, 1998		Colombia, Venezuela
Aug. 11, 1999	India	

1. The eclipse that will occur on August 11, 1999 will be seen from the

   _____ Hemisphere.

2. Write the names of the countries from which an eclipse was seen on March

   18, 1988. _____

3. An eclipse was seen from Finland. What was the date on which it happened?

Reading and Thinking

Complete each sentence with the correct word or words from the story.

1. Earth _____ the sun.

2. A solar eclipse happens when the moon

   goes between the _____

   and the _____ .

3. Check the main idea of the story.

   ____ learning about the earth's atmosphere

   ____ learning about eclipses

   ____ photographing an eclipse

4. Put **F** before the sentences that are facts. Put **O** before the sentences that are opinions.

   ____ Solar eclipses are more common than lunar eclipses.

   ____ A solar eclipse is nature's best show.

   ____ The moon orbits the earth.

   ____ We should all watch an eclipse.

5. Read paragraph 2 from the story. Summarize the important information of the paragraph in one sentence.

   _____

   _____

Working with Words

Rewrite each group of words below. Use possessive forms.

1. the suit of the astronaut

   _____

2. the shadow of the sun

   _____

Star Gazers

In this story, you'll learn important facts about stars.

1   "Meg," Uncle Max said one day, "I understand you've decided you'd like to write your science report about the stars. The *Bulletin* prints a night-sky map once a month. It shows what stars will be visible and in what positions the stars will be during that month. Why don't we go down to the *Bulletin* and look at this month's map?"

2   "Thanks, Uncle Max!" Meg exclaimed. "I was going to ask for your help. Let me get my coat and say good-bye to Mom."

3   On their way to the *Bulletin,* Uncle Max said, "Did you know that farmers in ancient times watched the stars to know when to plant their crops? I've been reading an astronomy book, and it contains a lot of interesting facts about stars."

4   "In the first chapter," Uncle Max went on, "I read that most stars, like our sun, are born inside a cloud of gas and dust. A star can shine so brightly because atomic energy makes these gases very hot. The star keeps shining until it runs out of hydrogen. That's the gas that is used to make atomic energy. After losing this gas, the star may explode. Then it returns to its cloud form of gas and dust."

5   "How long do most stars last?" asked Meg.

6   "Most stars have enough hydrogen to last over a billion years," Uncle Max answered.

7   "How many stars do you suppose are up there?" asked Meg as she pointed to the sky.

8   "My book says that there are more than one hundred billion stars in our galaxy, the Milky Way," answered Uncle Max.

9   "How many stars do you think will be visible tonight?" Meg asked.

10   "Well, since the sky is so clear, we'll probably be able to see about two thousand stars. Since astronomers sometimes use very large telescopes, they can see about three billion stars. Without a telescope, however, we can see only the brightest stars."

11   "Do the stars move?" Meg asked.

12   "Yes," Uncle Max answered, "but not in the same way we think they move. The stars, like our sun, seem to rise in the east and set in the west. However, the stars are so far away from the earth, we can't see them in motion. The sun, the closest star to the earth, moves about twelve miles per second. The sun and all the other stars in the Milky Way spin around the galaxy's center."

13   Meg asked, "Since I have a lot more to learn about stars before I write my report, may I use your astronomy book?"

14   "Of course," said Uncle Max. "It's on the bookshelf in my office. We'll pick it up when we get to the *Bulletin.*"

Photograph by Commerical Image

Knowing the Words

Write the words from the story that have the meanings below.

1. energy made from split atoms

_____
(Par. 4)

2. colorless gas that burns

_____
(Par. 4)

3. one thousand million

_____
(Par. 6)

4. Write a simile to describe the appearance of the stars in the sky. Remember to use *like* or *as* in your description.

_____

_____

In each row below, circle the three words that belong together.

5. sun   stars   grass   moon

6. galaxy   Saturn   Milky Way   boat

7. month   day   year   east

Learning to Study

Complete the following outline.

I. The life of the stars

   A. _____

   B. _____

   C. _____

II. The motion of the stars

   A. _____

   B. _____

   C. _____

Reading and Thinking

1. Where does a star begin? _____

_____

2. What is needed to make atomic energy?

_____

3. Our galaxy is known as _____ .

4. The main idea of paragraph 4 is

   ____ telescopes.

   ____ the life of a star.

   ____ the Milky Way.

5. Long ago people observed the night sky to tell time. How did the movement of the stars show the time of night?

_____

_____

6. Uncle Max knew a great deal about the

stars because _____

_____ .

Working with Words

You remember that the suffix **-ation** means "state, condition, action, or process of." Add **-ation** to each word. Then use the new word in a sentence. You may have to drop the final *e* before you add the suffix.

1. reserve _____

_____

2. accuse _____

_____

3. The suffix **-ion** can mean "state, condition, action, or process of." What does the word *addition* mean?

_____

63

A Visit to Washington, D.C.

Read this story to learn about Washington, D.C.

1 For their spring vacation, Mrs. Ellis, Uncle Max, Tom, and Meg went to Washington, D.C. On the first day of their visit, they took a tour of the city.

2 As the bus got rolling, their guide said, "I'm glad you've joined us this morning. My name is Clare. To start, let me tell you how this great city came to be.

3 "No one could agree where to locate the capital. To solve the problem, ten acres on the Potomac River were set aside in 1790 for the United States government. The area was named the District of Columbia. George Washington had the job of raising funds to buy the land and put up its buildings. He chose Major Pierre Charles L'Enfant as his city planner. Today, the city covers sixty-nine square miles. Many of the city's people work for the United States government.

4 "We are now passing the Capitol. It is well known for its rotunda, or round room. This round room has a large dome. A bronze Statue of Freedom stands on top of the dome. Few people realize that a tomb for George Washington lies beneath the

rotunda. However, Washington wanted to be buried at Mt. Vernon, his home, so the tomb is empty."

5 "How many rooms does the Capitol have?" asked Tom.

6 "The Capitol has five hundred forty rooms," Clare answered. "Many of the rooms contain lovely paintings and sculptures. A lot of people visit the Capitol to enjoy its beauty. But did you know that you can also attend sessions of Congress? Of course, you must first get a pass from one of the persons who represent you."

7 The tour went on. The next stop was the Supreme Court Building.

8 "Is this where the Supreme Court judges meet?" asked Meg.

9 "Yes," Clare said. "You may attend sessions of the court here as you can at the Capitol, but seating here is quite limited."

10 "We owe this building to William Howard Taft, who was Chief Justice and our twenty-seventh President. It was Taft who got Congress to build a new court building," Uncle Max whispered to Meg. "Mrs. Taft, by the way, helped get the city's famous cherry trees from the mayor of Tokyo."

11 "We'll cross Memorial Bridge now. We're going to visit Arlington Cemetery," Clare said. "Soldiers from nearly every American war are buried there. So are leaders such as President John F. Kennedy and his brother Robert. I also want to show you the memorial for the astronauts from the space shuttle *Challenger*. It has pictures of the seven astronauts who died in 1986."

12 After Tom and his family had completed the tour, Tom said, "Let's take the tour of the White House tomorrow. I told Lance and Betsy I'd take some pictures for them."

13 "That sounds good to me," Mrs. Ellis said. "We'll get an early start in the morning."

Knowing the Words

Write the words from the story that have the meanings below.

1. a large, round roof or ceiling

_____
(Par. 4)

2. highest rank

_____
(Par. 7)

3. a judge

_____
(Par. 10)

4. place where people are buried

_____
(Par. 11)

5. What abbreviation in the story stands for District of Columbia? _____

6. What is the abbreviation for United States? _____

Learning to Study

Here is a copy of Tom's airline ticket. Read it and answer the questions.

SUN AIRLINES
Name of Passenger
Tom Ellis

	Flight	**Date**	**Time**
From: Kendall	406	4/17	6:00 P.M.
Arriving: Washington, D.C.		4/17	9:00 P.M.
Ticket Number:	005 321 685		

1. What time will Tom leave Kendall?

_____

2. On what date will he fly? _____

3. On what airline will Tom fly?

_____

Reading and Thinking

1. How many rooms are in the Capitol?

_____

2. Who planned the city of Washington, D.C.?

_____

3. Washington, D.C., covers how many square miles? _____

4. Put **B** before the phrases that describe Washington before it was finished. Put **A** before the phrases that describe the city after it was finished.

_____ muddy, torn up ground

_____ no paved streets

_____ half-finished government offices

_____ trees and gardens on the White House grounds

5. Write one fact Tom learned about the Capitol. _____

_____

6. Write an opinion that Tom may have formed after visiting the Capitol.

_____

_____

Working with Words

After reading each sentence, write the compound word that correctly fills each blank.

1. Meg packed a _____ before she left for vacation.   (suitcase, mailbox)

2. We arrived at the _____ just as the plane took off.   (sidewalk, airport)

3. Has _____ seen my airline ticket?   (everywhere, anyone)

The White House Tour

Read this story. Then decide whether you would like to tour the White House.

1   On the second day of their vacation in Washington, D.C., Tom and his family toured the White House. Meg and Tom were looking forward to seeing the home of the President of the United States.

2   "The White House is actually made of sandstone," explained Lea, the tour guide. "In the beginning, it was painted white to make it look like marble. It's been painted white ever since. Most pictures show the building from the north side, where it seems to be a two-story structure. The White House, however, really has four stories."

3   Lea took Tom and the rest of the visitors to the East Room.

4   "Look up there," Meg said, pointing to the ceiling. Hanging from the ceiling were three crystal chandeliers that looked like frozen fountains.

5   Lea told everyone that the East Room has had many uses. "Important people from all over the world have been in this room. But this room hasn't always been used for entertaining," Lea added. "Back in 1800, many White House rooms were not finished. Abigail Adams was the first wife of a president to live in the White House. She needed the East Room to hang her laundry."

6   Toward the end of the tour, Meg said, "I was hoping we could see the President."

7   "Many people say that," Lea explained. "Most tourists see only the first two floors of the White House. The President and the President's family spend most of their time in private rooms on the third floor."

8   "What's on the third floor?" Tom asked.

9   "On the third floor, there are offices, a sitting room, a library, and living space," Lea answered.

10   "Once when I was on assignment," Uncle Max said, "I got to see the Lincoln Room,

which is on the third floor. There is a seven-foot bed that was specially made for Lincoln. The handwork was beautiful! I also saw a very interesting table."

11   "I know about that table," Meg said. "My teacher showed us a picture of it. Its four legs curve in toward one another. Where the legs meet is a wooden nest that holds four wooden eggs."

12   "Has the building changed much over the years?" Mrs. Ellis asked.

13   "Many additions have been made to the main building of the White House," Lea said. "A dentist's office, a doctor's office, a swimming pool, a gym, and even a movie theater have been added. The main building, though, has not changed its appearance for many years."

14   "I didn't realize the White House was so big," Tom said as the tour ended. "Maybe someday I'll come back here as a reporter covering a big story."

15   "You just might do that," said Mrs. Ellis. "Meanwhile, let's get back to the hotel to pack. We don't want to miss our flight home."

Photograph courtesy of White House Historical Association

Knowing the Words

Write the words from the story that have the meanings below.

1. a type of glass

   _____
   (Par. 4)

2. visitors

   _____
   (Par. 7)

3. in a special manner

   _____
   (Par. 10)

4. way something looks

   _____
   (Par. 13)

5. What is the simile in paragraph 4?

   _____

   _____

Learning to Study

Read the dictionary entry and answer the questions below.

pres i dent /prez´ə dənt/ *n* the chief officer of a company, college, club, or society

1. Would the word *press* come before or

   after *president*? _____

2. What part of speech is *president*?

   _____

3. Write the word *president* in syllables.

   _____

4. Write two guide words that might appear on the dictionary page where *president* is found.

   _____

Reading and Thinking

Put **T** before each sentence that is true. Put **F** before each sentence that is false.

1. ____ Most photographs show the south side of the White House.

2. ____ Crystal chandeliers hang in the East Room.

3. ____ The Lincoln Room is located on the first floor.

4. ____ The President and the President's family live on the third floor.

5. The main idea of paragraph 2 is

   _____

   _____.

Write the word that best completes each sentence.

6. You certainly are _____ to a long vacation.

   entitled   continued   concentrated

7. The group will _____ a map to the White House.

   encourage   rescue   provide

8. Do you think Tom will visit the White House again? Why or why not?

   _____

   _____

Working with Words

The suffix **-an** means "one who is from." For example, an American is someone "who is from America." Use **-an** to form a word that correctly completes each sentence.

1. One who is from Asia is _____.

2. One who is from Ohio is an _____.

3. One who is from Hawaii is a _____.

Mark Twain

Read this story to learn some important facts about a great writer.

1 "I'm told this actor we've come to see almost convinces you that he is Mark Twain. This should make quite a feature story for both of us," said Uncle Max as he and Tom took their seats in the theater.

2 "Huckleberry Finn will always be my hero," Tom said. "He had some great adventures. Every time I read that book, I wish I could've been there with him."

3 "I've always dreamed of rafting down a river," Uncle Max admitted. "I'd look up at the stars at night just like Huck and his friend Jim did," whispered his uncle as the curtain rose.

4 On the stage stood a gentleman all clad in white, right down to his shoes. Bushy white hair crowned his head, and he sported a full, rich, white moustache.

5 "My, my, look at all these fine folks who've come to see me," the actor's voice boomed. "You know, I was born Samuel Clemens, and there's nothing wrong with that name. I just found it a bit dull, so I took my name from the river I adored. You see, when that old steamboat came chugging along the Mississippi River, everyone listened for the call, 'mark twain.' I loved the sound of it. That meant the river had been measured at two fathoms, or twelve feet. In other words, it was just deep enough for a steamboat to pass through.

6 "You know, I left school when I was twelve. I don't recommend it, but I have no regrets. I've been a printer's helper and a riverboat pilot. I even went west looking for gold, but since I found nothing but rock, I started writing for a newspaper."

7 The performance went on as the man told stories about life on the Mississippi River. Some of the stories were funny, but they all seemed to have a special message.

8 "Some folks think I'm funny, although some say I poke too much fun at people. I say it's good to be noble. But to tell others how to be good is nobler and less trouble. And why shouldn't we laugh at ourselves? I mean, let's face it. People are the only animals who blush—and the only ones that need to!"

9 The audience clapped then, as they recognized Mark Twain's famous quote.

10 The actor closed by saying, "You know, I came in with Halley's Comet in 1835. The comet is coming again soon and I'd sure be disappointed if I didn't go out with it. I'm looking forward to that. And now, goodnight."

11 Applause filled the auditorium. As the actor who looked so much like Mark Twain stepped from the stage, a voice was heard saying, "Halley's Comet, which appears every seventy-five years or so, showed up during the week of Mark Twain's death."

12 "What a great performance!" Tom exclaimed. "I want to start on my story right away, before I forget anything."

13 "You're right. We've got work to do," Uncle Max said, "so let's go."

Knowing the Words

Write the words from the story that have the meanings below.

1. special article

_____
(Par. 1)

2. dressed

_____
(Par. 4)

3. measurement of depth

_____
(Par. 5)

4. a bright, starlike heavenly body

_____
(Par. 10)

5. Write **A** between each pair of words that are antonyms, words with opposite meanings.

always _____ never

friend _____ enemy

helper _____ assistant

dull _____ exciting

clap _____ applaud

Learning to Study

Write the number of the encyclopedia volume that would have the most information for each of the topics below.

Vol.	Vol.	Vol,	Vol.	Vol.	Vol.	Vol.
1	2	3	4	5	6	7
A–C	D–F	G–J	K–M	N–Q	R–T	U–Z

1. Mississippi River _____

2. Samuel L. Clemens _____

3. Steamboats _____

4. Halley's Comet _____

5. *Tom Sawyer* _____

Reading and Thinking

1. Mark Twain's real name was _____

_____.

2. How many feet equal two fathoms?

_____

3. The main idea of paragraph 6 is

_____ looking for gold.

_____ Mark Twain's various jobs.

_____ Halley's Comet.

Write the word that best completes each sentence.

4. I hope the raft doesn't _____ when we are on the lake.

clutch   overturn   shiver

5. A person needs good _____ skills to be an actor.

communication   feature   comet

Working with Words

The prefix **im-** sometimes means "not." Add **im-** to each word. Then write its new meaning.

1. polite _____

_____

2. perfect _____

_____

3. possible _____

_____

4. patient _____

_____

5. The prefix **il-** can also mean "not." Write a definition for the word *illegal.*

_____

69

A Family Tree

In this story, you'll discover how to make a family tree.

1 "How many of you have ever tried to trace your ancestors?" Miss Todd asked her history class one day.

2 Several students raised their hands, and Tom said, "Miss Todd, I've always wanted to know more about my family's history. The thing is, I've never know how to find out."

3 "I'm glad you brought that up, Tom," Miss Todd replied. "That's what we're going to talk about today." Then turning to the rest of the class, Miss Todd went on, "We are about to set off on a study of the generations that came before us."

4 "Isn't that what Alex Haley did when he wrote the book *Roots?*" Susan asked.

5 "Yes," Miss Todd answered. "He went back to Africa and discovered his ancestor Kunta Kinte. Haley's book made many people think about tracing their roots. Now, I'd like to tell you about my search for my roots."

6 "Where did you begin?" Tom asked.

7 "First, I talked with my parents and grandparents. They were a good source of information. My aunts and uncles helped, too. Some of my relatives had saved some interesting photographs. In fact, I even found a diary and some old letters."

8 "My grandfather left a journal of his voyage to America," Susan said. "He talked about the people he left behind. He wrote about the Statue of Liberty and Ellis Island, too."

9 "Ellis Island is where immigrants were checked and cleared before they could enter this country," Miss Todd explained. "My grandmother was an immigrant from Poland. When she came through Ellis Island's gates, she'd left behind many of her family's records. Therefore, it was quite hard to trace her roots. You know," Miss Todd went on, "many of your relatives passed through Ellis Island's gates, too. That's something we should know about."

10 "What did you do after you talked with your relatives?'" Betsy asked.

11 "I used my notes to make a chart. I started with my birthplace and birthdate. Then I drew connecting lines to my parents, then my grandparents, and so on. I wrote their birthplaces, dates of birth, and if and when they came to the United States."

12 "What did you do when you couldn't go any further?" Tom asked.

13 "I wrote to a library in Salt Lake City, Utah. It helps people trace their roots. It has the world's largest and most complete collection of these facts. It also has 2650 branch libraries. They are in the United States, Canada, and sixty-two other countries. If some of you would like the address, you can see me after class. Anyway, I sent the library what I'd gathered, and it helped me find out more. You see, the more investigation you do, the better your family tree will be. Monday, I'll bring in my own family tree so you can see the finished product. Now, let's finish reviewing for Friday's exam."

Knowing the Words

Write the words from the story that have the meanings below.

1. relatives of long ago

_____
(Par. 1)

2. book or journal for personal writing

_____
(Par. 7)

3. people who are new to a country

_____
(Par. 9)

4. Write this address without abbreviations.

Dr. Sarah Jenkins
50 E. North Temple St.
Salt Lake City, UT 84150

_____

_____

_____

Working with Words

Rewrite each group of words below using possessive forms.

1. the diary that belongs to Kim

_____

2. the book that Alex owns

_____

3. the office used by two dentists

_____

4. the windows of a truck

_____

5. the library used by the students

_____

Reading and Thinking

1. What are Tom and his classmates going to make? _____

2. Who wrote the book called *Roots?*

_____

3. The author wrote this story to

____ inform readers about studying family history.

____ discuss the book *Roots*.

____ invite people to Salt Lake City, Utah.

4. Why did Miss Todd look at old letters?

_____

_____

5. Read paragraph 7 from the story. Summarize the important information of the paragraph in one sentence.

_____

_____

_____

Learning to Study

Look at the timeline and answer the questions below.

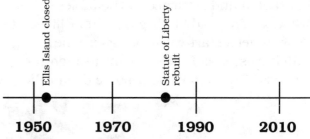

1. How many years does the line between each pair of dates stand for? _____

2. Between which two dates did the rebuilding of the Statue of Liberty take place? _____

Tie-Dyeing

Tie-dyeing is a way of decorating cloth. Read this story to learn how it's done.

1   "OK, everyone," Susan said, "we want this to be the best junior class picnic ever. But it can't be unless each of us makes something that's good enough to sell at the school bazaar. Tom's mom, Mrs. Ellis, has agreed to teach us how to tie-dye. She's here now to tell us how it's done. Mrs. Ellis, we're all yours."

2   "Thank you, Susan. I'm glad to be here to help you with this project. Tie-dyeing is really not hard," Mrs. Ellis began. "It's a simple way to decorate cloth with a variety of patterns made from spots, circles, spirals, and patches.

3   "In its simplest form, cloth is tied in tight knots. The knots prevent dye from penetrating them. This method creates wild, irregular patterns when the cloth is unknotted. You'll be tie-dyeing scarves, T-shirts, handkerchiefs, and tablecloths. I have brought all the materials you'll need.

4   "I think it would be best if you work in groups. Each group should fill one pan with warm water and another pan with very hot water. Place each pan on sheets of newspaper to protect the tables."

5   The students filled the pans as instructed and returned to the tables. "Now, you're ready to begin," Mrs. Ellis said. "Susan, let's start with you. Everyone watch closely as I take Susan through the process. OK, Susan, pour some dye in the very hot water and stir it with one of these sticks. Try not to put your hands in the dye. Now wet your scarf in the clear water and squeeze it out. Next, pick a spot on your wet scarf, bunch the scarf together, and put a rubber band around it."

6   "Just one?" Susan asked uncertainly.

7   "You can use several rubber bands if you wish, as long as the bands are tight. You can make one big circle or several small ones," Mrs. Ellis replied.

8   "OK, Susan, now put your scarf in the dye and stir the water until your scarf is a little darker than you want it. Use the stick to remove it."

9   "What's next?" asked Susan as she held the stick with both hands.

10   "You're ready to rinse the scarf in your pan of clear water," Mrs. Ellis said. "Get clean water if you need to. OK, everyone, that's all there is to tie-dyeing. When you're all done, let your cloth dry, but don't put it out in the sun or try to iron it too quickly because the color will fade.

11   "Tomorrow, we'll remove all the rubber bands. If you made scarves, handkerchiefs, or tablecloths, you'll need to hem them. If you've tie-dyed a T-shirt, you're already done!"

Knowing the Words

Write the words from the story that have the meanings below.

1. place to sell many different items

_____
(Par. 1)

2. winding shapes

_____
(Par. 2)

3. soaking through

_____
(Par. 3)

4. uneven

_____
(Par. 3)

5. Write **S** between each pair of words that are synonyms, words with similar meanings.

best	_____	worst
now	_____	immediately
simple	_____	easy
irregular	_____	uneven

Learning to Study

Complete this outline.

I. Things to do before tie-dying

   A. _____

   B. _____

   C. _____

   D. _____

II. Things to do during tie-dying

   A. _____

   B. _____

   C. _____

   D. _____

Reading and Thinking

1. Number the events to show the order in which they happened.

_____ Susan introduced Mrs. Ellis.

_____ Susan rinsed out her cloth.

_____ Each group filled pans with water.

_____ Susan put a rubber band around the cloth.

_____ Susan put the cloth into the dye.

2. Why did Mrs. Ellis warn Susan not to put her hands in the dye? _____

_____

_____

3. Read paragraph 2 from the story. Summarize the important information of the paragraph in one sentence.

_____

_____

4. Each group of students placed the pans of water on newspaper because _____

_____ .

Working with Words

The prefix **mis-** means "badly" or "the opposite of." For example, the word *mistreat* means "to treat badly." Add **mis-** to each word in parentheses to complete the sentence.

1. Juan _____ the map that was upside down. (read)

2. The child was _____ in the store. (behaving)

3. Julie _____ her new pair of shoes. (placed)

Edison, the Great Inventor

Read this story to learn about Tom and Lance's project for the school Interest Fair.

1 The Kendall High Interest Fair was only two weeks away, and the school was buzzing with excitement. The Interest Fair was an annual event that gave students an opportunity to share their hobbies or show off their abilities in many areas of interest. Some students were still doing research for their projects. Others were sewing, building, or crafting their projects.

2 Tom and Lance were working together on a project. Because of their interest in inventors, the two boys planned a trip to Milan, Ohio, where Thomas Edison was born. Tom and Lance left on Saturday.

3 Staring out of the bus window, Lance nudged Tom and pointed to a road sign. "At last, we're here! 'Welcome to Milan, Ohio, birthplace of Thomas Alva Edison.'"

4 "It's hard to believe that Edison went to school for only three months," Tom said. "He gave us so much."

5 "Apparently, he was so curious about so many subjects that his mother decided to teach him herself. His mother must have been one fine teacher, I'd say!" Lance remarked.

6 Tom and Lance picked up a tour book and joined the crowd in the Exhibit Hall.

7 "Here's the first thing Edison tried to sell," said Lance, aiming his camera at Edison's 1868 vote recorder. "He invented this when he was just twenty-one!"

8 "The card says it was the first voting machine," said Tom.

9 "Look at this!" Lance exclaimed. "This phonograph was an invention he was very proud of. The first words heard were, 'Mary had a little lamb.'"

10 Lance snapped picture after picture. Tom quickly took notes. "You know, he developed one of the first motion picture cameras," Tom said. "He also improved the phone to carry voices over long distances."

11 Next Tom and Lance reached Edison's light bulb. A guide said. "Edison's greatest experiments were with the electric light. A type of electric bulb called an arc light had already been in use, but it was too bright. No one could use it indoors. Edison invented a light bulb for indoor use. It held a special wire. When electricity heated that wire, light was given off. The light bulbs we use today are much like the one Edison gave us in 1879."

12 "After that invention, he was called 'The Wizard of Menlo Park.' His famous lab is there, in New Jersey," Lance added.

13 Tom and Lance looked at all the displays honoring Edison. Their respect for him grew. The inventions they saw included everything from telegraphs to storage batteries.

14 "What a genius!" Tom exclaimed as Lance reloaded his camera. "No wonder people believe he was the greatest inventor in history. By the time he died in 1931, he'd been awarded 1,093 patents!"

Knowing the Words

Write the words from the story that have the meanings below.

1. it seems that

_____
(Par. 5)

2. a curved spark of electricity

_____
(Par. 11)

3. very intelligent person

_____
(Par. 14)

4. permits given for inventions

_____
(Par. 14)

5. Check the sentence in which *carry* has the same meaning it does in paragraph 10.

_____ Rosa can't carry a tune.

_____ An actor's voice must carry to the last row of seats.

_____ Please carry my coat to the bus.

Learning to Study

Libraries arrange biographies in alphabetical order. They use the last name of the person who is the subject of the book. Number these biographies to show their order on a library shelf.

1. _____ *The Life of Thomas Jefferson*

2. _____ *Thomas A. Edison, Inventor*

3. _____ *Marie Curie, Scientist*

4. _____ *Up in Space With Sally Ride*

5. Check the subjects you could look up to learn more about Thomas Edison.

_____ electric lights   _____ mountains

_____ phonographs   _____ newspapers

_____ flags   _____ light bulb

Reading and Thinking

1. When did Edison invent his light bulb?

_____

2. How old was Edison when he invented his vote recorder? _____

3. Check the main idea of the story.

_____ making long-distance calls

_____ a famous inventor

_____ the light bulb

4. Why was Edison called "The Wizard of Menlo Park"? _____

_____

_____

5. The arc light couldn't be used indoors because _____.

6. Why is Thomas Edison known as the greatest inventor in history?

_____

_____

_____

Working with Words

To make a plural word that does not end in *s* show ownership, add *'s*. For example, *the toys of the children* could be written *the children's toys*. Rewrite each group of words below. Use possessive forms.

1. sound of the geese _____

2. homes for the deer _____

3. gloves of the women _____

4. wool of the sheep _____

5. tails of the mice _____

Native Americans

Read this story to learn about what life was like long ago.

1   Tom and Lance were leaving school one day. "What are you going to write about for your final history paper, Lance?" Tom asked.

2   "My ancestors were members of the Plains Indians," Lance said. "I thought I'd write about their tribe. I've been reading about their sign language. It's really fascinating! Here were all of these different tribes on the Plains, each with its own way of communicating. But when they met one another, they could talk by using hand signals. Sometimes members of the same tribe used these signals so they wouldn't be overheard. But mostly, they used them when talking with members of other tribes. It was handy when the tribes had to settle differences and make trade agreements. Anyway, that's what I think I'll write about. How about you?"

3   "I might do a general study of Indians," Tom said.

4   "Don't you mean 'Native Americans'?" Lance asked curiously.

5   "Well, you know there never were true natives in the New World. We're all immigrants. Even those people who met Christopher Columbus were immigrants. He called them *Indians* because he thought he was in the Indies. He was wrong about that, of course. The people he called Indians originally came from Asia. Do you know how they got here, Lance?" Tom asked.

6   "I think I did read something about that. I think the book I read said that over twenty thousand years ago, an ice age created a land bridge," Lance said. "It joined Siberia with what is now Alaska. That's how these first people came here. They weren't trying to discover a new land, like Columbus. They were just following the animals they hunted. They depended on them to live. If the animals moved, the people had to follow."

7   "That's right," Tom continued. "As time went by, they spread out everywhere from Alaska to the tip of South America. Every time they reached a new area, they met up with lots of animals they'd never seen before. They must have had all kinds of adventures."

8   "I know what you mean," Lance agreed. "Can you imagine what it must have been like to walk fifty miles or more in search of food with just arrows and spears for protection?"

9   "I wonder if we could survive in the wilderness," Tom said.

10   "Well, we'd have to learn to hunt," Lance said. "We'd also have to learn to protect ourselves from wild animals. Let's not try living in the wilderness yet. We've got a lot more reading to do first!" Lance said as he and Tom headed for the library.

Knowing the Words

Write the words from the story that have the meanings below.

1. very interesting

_____
(Par. 2)

2. convenient

_____
(Par. 2)

3. understandings between tribes

_____
(Par. 2)

Circle the word with the correct meaning in each sentence below.

4. Anne decided to (write, right) a letter to her uncle.

5. Have you (scene, seen) my book about Sioux Indians?

Learning to Study

This is a map of some midwestern states. The map also shows the area where the Plains Indians lived. Look at the map and answer the questions below.

1. The Plains stretched from the Mississippi River on the east to the

_____ on the west.

2. Is Nebraska north or south of Kansas?

_____

Reading and Thinking

1. Lance's ancestors were _____ Indians.

2. What two areas were connected by a land bridge?

_____

3. Why did the people cross the land

bridge? _____

_____

4. Why did different tribes on the Plains use hand signals to communicate?

_____

_____

Write the word that best completes each sentence.

5. Lance _____ many new facts about living in the wilderness.

discovered   traveled   attached

6. High waves made the sea too _____ for sailing.

lucky   rough   careful

7. What might have happened if the people hadn't crossed the land bridge

into Alaska? _____

_____

Working with Words

After reading each sentence, write the compound word that correctly fills each blank.

1. Yoko found _____ on the beach this morning. (seashells, rainbows)

2. I watched a lovely _____ from my hotel room. (suntan, sunset)

Floating on Air

Read this story to learn about some great moments in the history of ballooning.

1   The Montgolfier brothers invented the hot-air balloon in 1783. However, they probably never guessed how high or how far one of these balloons could go. In the brothers' first demonstration, they used a huge bag made of paper and fabric. They held its open end over a fire. The bag filled with smoke and hot air. Then it rose into the air and floated for a mile and a half.

2   No one rode in these first balloons. The balloons didn't even have baskets under them for passengers. Yet airplanes were still to be invented, and people were eager to fly. Hot-air balloons offered the first real opportunity for air travel.

3   Since then, the balloons have become much safer. Their baskets not only hold passengers, but also special instruments to help control the flight. Ballooning has become a hobby for some. For others, it offers an exciting challenge.

4   Jetta Schantz took her first balloon ride as a birthday present. Ten years later, she was setting ballooning records. In February 1996, the 36-year-old Schantz set a new women's record by staying in the air for 15 hours, 11 minutes. The old record of 11 hours, 10 minutes, had been set in 1974.

5   That was not Schantz's first record. In 1993 she broke the women's distance record and in 1994 she broke nine world records by taking a balloon 32,657 feet into the air. At that height, the air temperature drops to -40° F. The icy air froze her flight instruments.

6   As Schantz rose higher and higher, the amount of oxygen in the air dropped. A balloon's burners need oxygen to stay lighted. Schantz went so high that the lack of oxygen put out her burners. Then the air inside the balloon quickly cooled. The balloon fell, out of control, to 18,000 feet. At that point, Schantz was able to re-light the burners and land safely.

7   For setting the world altitude record, Schantz received an international award named for the brothers who invented ballooning. Schantz's achievement was also listed as one of the ten most memorable flights of 1994.

8   Having broken 27 world records, ballooning has taken Schantz from celebrating her birthday to being celebrated. She says, "All my life I wanted to accomplish something. These awards show that no dream is too big."

Photograph courtesy of Curt Goenen/North Light Studios

Knowing the Words

Write the words from the story that have the meanings below.

1. cloth

_____
(Par. 1)

2. height

_____
(Par. 7)

3. worth remembering

_____
(Par. 7)

4. You have learned that idioms are groups of words that have special meanings. What does the idiom *in the clouds* mean?

_____

_____

_____

Working with Words

The suffix **-ous** usually means "full of" or "having." The suffix **-ous** can be added to nouns to change them to adjectives. Add the suffix **-ous** to these nouns. Then use each new word in a sentence.

1. thunder _____

_____

2. humor _____

_____

Write the noun and suffix that form each adjective.

adjective	noun	suffix
3. courageous	_____	_____
4. poisonous	_____	_____

Reading and Thinking

1. Why did the first hot-air balloons just drift in the wind? _____

_____

2. Why could Schantz re-light the burners after the balloon dropped to 18,000 feet?

_____

3. What hot-air ballooning records has Schantz set? _____

_____

_____

4. Number the events to show the order in which they happened.

_____ Jetta Schantz set the hot-air balloon altitude record.

_____ The Montgolfier brothers demonstrated their balloon.

_____ Schantz set a record for staying up in the air in a balloon.

_____ Schantz received an award named after the Montgolfier brothers.

_____ Flight instruments began to be used in hot-air balloons.

Learning to Study

Complete this partial outline.

I. Important events in Jetta Schantz's life.

  A. _____

  B. _____

  _____

  C. _____

  _____

Write a newspaper caption for the photo on page 78. _____

_____

A Visit to the Veterinarian

In this story, Meg learns more about a veterinarian's job.

1   It was the end of the school year. To finish their study unit on animals, Meg's teacher Ms. Cheng arranged a trip for her class. They would meet Dr. Renée Collins, a local veterinarian.

2   Dr. Collins' assistant Luis greeted the students. "Before we go in, I must warn you. Several people have brought their pets in today. The animals will be quite nervous about seeing the doctor. Some animals howl and some shake. Some even try to drag their owners right back out the door. Now come with me into the waiting room. You'll see what I mean."

3   As he led them to the waiting room, Luis began, "This isn't a typical doctor's office with carpeting and comfortable chairs. You'll notice we use wooden seats. The flooring is ceramic tile. Some of our animals have accidents," he laughed. "Because of that, we had to pull up the rugs that were once here."

4   Next, Luis led the class into one of the examining rooms. "It looks just like the one in my doctor's office," Meg whispered.

5   "Yes, but look at that metal examining table!" Kate remarked.

6   Everyone watched quietly as Dr. Collins came in with a white poodle and its owner. "There, there, Casey," she reassured the dog. Then Dr. Collins gently placed the dog on the table.

7   "These sores you're worried about are caused by an allergy," Dr. Collins explained to the dog's owner. "Now, dogs don't cough and sneeze the way humans do. In dogs, allergies show up through their skin. It makes them itch like crazy! Often, an allergy is caused by a flea bite, but I think these sores are caused by something in the air or something she's eaten or touched.

Can you think of any changes that might have affected Casey?"

8   "Could the new dog food I've been feeding her cause the allergy?" asked Casey's owner.

9   "It certainly could. Go back to what she's used to eating," Dr. Collins advised. "In the meantime, I'll give her a shot that should make her feel better. If the sores haven't healed by next week, stop by and we'll run some tests."

10   After the owner left with her dog, Dr. Collins addressed the students. "Animals get sick and hurt just as we do. Sometimes, I have to perform surgery. After surgery, some animals have to stay in our hospital for a time. We also board healthy pets when their families go on vacation. That's why you hear that barking," she laughed.

11   "What made you become a veterinarian?" Ms. Cheng asked.

12   "I grew up on a farm and have cared for animals all my life. Animals provide such companionship. Quite simply, I love them," Dr. Collins answered.

Knowing the Words

Write the words from the story that have the meanings below.

1. usual kind

   _____
   (Par. 3)

2. a floor covering

   _____
   (Par. 3)

3. renewed or restored confidence

   _____
   (Par. 6)

4. Write **S** between each pair of words that are synonyms, words with similar meanings.

   helper   _____   assistant

   nervous   _____   calm

   doctor   _____   physician

   gently   _____   roughly

   remain   _____   stay

   healthy   _____   well

Learning to Study

Complete this outline.

   I. _____

      A. Choosing the right pet

      B. Training your pet

   II. _____

      A. Getting your pet's shots

      B. Getting enough food and exercise

The yellow pages of the phone book provide helpful information when you need a phone number or an address. For example, if you needed a place for your pet to stay while you were on vacation, you could look in the yellow pages under the topic **kennels.** Suppose you needed a place to take your pet when it got sick. Under what topic could you look?

_____

Reading and Thinking

Put **F** before each sentence that is a fact.
Put **O** before each sentence that is an opinion.

1. _____ Cats make better pets than dogs.

2. _____ Many pets provide companionship.

3. _____ Some veterinarians board animals for pet owners who are on vacation.

4. _____ All children want to own a dog.

5. Check the words below that describe Dr. Collins.

   _____ caring   _____ devoted

   _____ shy   _____ upset

6. The author wrote this story to

   _____ talk about pets.

   _____ tell what a veterinarian does.

   _____ tell you about Meg's class.

Working with Words

To make a plural word that ends in s show ownership, add just an apostrophe. Rewrite each group of words below. Add an apostrophe to the underlined word to show ownership. One is done for you.

the toys of the <u>babies</u>   **babies' toys**

1. the windows of the <u>stores</u>

   _____

2. the pencils that the <u>students</u> use

   _____

Rewrite each group of words below. Use possessive forms.

3. the coats that the men have

   _____

4. the feathers of the bird

   _____

A Day at the Zoo

Read this story and learn more about Betsy's and Nina's trip to the zoo.

1 Drenched from head to foot with rain, Betsy's friend Nina pulled the house key from her pocket and struggled to unlock the door. As she pushed it open, she heard the phone ringing. Quickly dropping her book bag, she raced to the kitchen and picked up the phone.

2 "Great weather, huh?" she heard Betsy ask. "You sound awful! Did I call at a bad time?"

3 "It depends on what you call bad," Nina muttered, shivering. Looking down, she noticed that her sneakers squirted water every time she wiggled her toes. "What's up, Betsy?"

4 "How does an afternoon at the zoo sound to you?"

5 "At the moment, it sounds rotten," Nina laughed, "but what did you have in mind?"

6 "For a photography course I'm taking at Kendall College, I have to photograph several zoo animals. I was wondering if you'd go with me on Saturday."

7 "As long as the weather improves, I don't see why not," Nina answered.

8 On Saturday, the bright sun greeted the girls. The frost was just beginning to melt when Nina picked up Betsy. Then off they went to the city zoo.

9 While Nina looked at the elephants, Betsy took photographs.

10 "Hey, Betsy," Nina said, "is that a new camera? I haven't seen it before."

11 "This is my single-lens reflex camera," Betsy said. "You've probably seen my range finder. I usually use that one when I'm taking photographs for my photo album. I brought my SLR today. I want to be able to change the camera lens."

12 "Can't you do that with the range finder?" Nina asked.

13 "No," Betsy answered. "With the SLR, I can get the detail of the animal because I can shoot close-up shots when I change to a longer lens. If I want to get some of the zoo background, I can use a wide-angle lens."

14 Betsy and Nina continued walking. Nina gazed at the giraffes mildly munching a few remaining leaves and said, "I've never been to the zoo at this time of the year. It's nice having the place almost to ourselves."

15 "You're right," Betsy said. "It's so quiet here. Let's finish up at the monkey house. I think I've got most of the shots I need, and besides, we're beginning to lose the light."

16 "This was a wonderful way to relax," Nina said as she and Betsy headed for the parking lot. "I bet your photos will be fantastic."

Knowing the Words

Write the words from the story that have the meanings below.

1. soaked

   _____
   (Par. 1)

2. part of a camera

   _____
   (Par. 11)

3. throw back an image

   _____
   (Par. 11)

4. a book to hold pictures

   _____
   (Par. 11)

5. **Personification** is a figure of speech in which an author talks about an idea or object as if it had lifelike qualities. Find the example of personification in paragraph 8 from the story.

   _____

Learning to Study

Read this dictionary entry. Answer the questions below.

al bum /al´ bəm/ *n* **1** book with blank pages for holding stamps, photographs, etc. **2** a single long-playing record

1. What syllable is stressed when *album* is pronounced? _____

2. Which definition gives the meaning of *album* as it is used in paragraph 11? ___

3. What part of speech is *album*? _____

4. Write the word *album* in syllables.

   _____

Reading and Thinking

1. Check the main idea of the story.

   ____ taking good photographs

   ____ collecting photos

   ____ getting soaked in the rain

2. During what season do you think the story takes place? _____

3. Why were there so few people at the zoo on the day that Betsy went to take pictures? _____

   _____

4. What is one difference between a range-finder camera and an SLR camera?

   _____

   _____

Working with Words

You remember that the prefix **re-** means "again" or "back." Write words that have the following meanings by adding the prefix **re-** to a base word. Then use the new word in a sentence.

1. fill again _____

   _____

2. turn back _____

   _____

The suffix **-ship** usually mean "a state or condition of being." Write the meaning of each word.

3. leadership _____

   _____

4. township _____

   _____

Summer Days

Read this story to discover why Tom and Betsy are heading into a great summer.

1 "Tom, I just had to call you right away! You'll never guess what I'll be doing this summer. I got the job!" shrieked Betsy excitedly into the phone.

2 "Hey, slow down, Bets. Tell me what you're talking about," Tom said.

3 "A few months ago, I wrote to a magazine, *Reflections,* asking about a summer job. I included some samples of my photographs with the letter. Last week, the editor interviewed me. Today, I heard from her again!"

4 "Congratulations, Betsy," said Tom proudly. "What kind of work will you be doing and when do you begin?"

5 "Are you ready for this? I start June fifteenth as a photojournalist. It's sort of like what I've been doing for the school paper," Betsy explained. "I use my camera to tell a story, instead of using a computer as you do. The difference is that *The Knightly News* uses just one or two of my photos to accompany it. At *Reflections,* they'll want me to do a complete photo essay."

6 "I know what you mean," Tom said. "With a series of pictures, you'll tell a story. You know, I read that it was *Life* magazine that made the photo essay a real part of modern journalism. How do you get started on a project?" Tom asked.

7 "It takes a lot of planning. First, I'll have to decide what kinds of pictures I'll need. Since it's somewhat like a written essay, there will be a beginning, middle, and end to my picture story. Some photos will serve as my opener, setting the mood of my essay. I'll need others to carry my main theme, and finally, I'll use some shots to finish up with," Betsy explained.

8 "It sounds as if you're ready to begin right now, Betsy. Congratulations! I'm really glad for you. I guess we'll both be busy this summer."

9 "When do you start your summer job at the *Bulletin?*" Betsy asked.

10 "At the end of June," Tom replied. "I'm really looking forward to it. It's not just because of the money I'll earn. It'll be so neat watching the reporters, editors, and crew put together an issue of *The Kendall Bulletin* every day. I'll be spending most of my time working with the make-up crew in the composing room. Then, right before I get ready to come back to school in September, I'll spend a few weeks covering stories with Uncle Max. I can hardly wait."

11 "We'll really make a great team on *The Knightly News* when we go back to school. Look out world, here we come!" Betsy exclaimed.

Knowing the Words

Write the words from the story that have the meanings below.

1. go along with

_____
(Par. 5)

2. story told with photographs

_____
(Par. 5)

3. several in a row

_____
(Par. 6)

Learning to Study

Look at this diagram of one kind of newspaper press and answer the questions below.

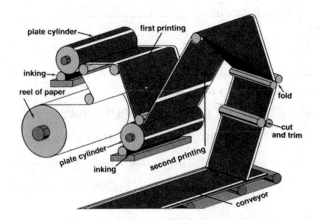

1. How many plate cylinders does the press

have? _____

2. After the paper is printed, it is then

_____ .

Complete the following partial outline.

I. Making a Photo Essay

   A. _____

   B. _____

Reading and Thinking

1. Why did Betsy send some of her photographs to the magazine?

_____

_____

2. Betsy isn't beginning her summer job until June fifteenth because _____

_____

_____ .

3. What part of his summer job do you think Tom will enjoy the most? Why?

_____

_____

4. Write one of the differences between a reporter and a photojournalist.

_____

_____

5. Write one sentence the author used to show how Betsy felt at the beginning of

the story. _____

_____

Working with Words

The prefix **sub-** can mean "under" or "below." For example, the word *subway* means a train that travels under the ground. Add **sub-** to each word. Then write its new meaning.

1. marine _____

_____

2. normal _____

_____

85

Checking Understanding

1. Number the events in the order in which they happened in the story.

_____ Ms. Lopez praises Tom's work.

_____ Tom meets with Ms. Lopez.

_____ Lance discusses the Festival.

_____ Betsy gets her assignment.

_____ Tom and Betsy wait to discuss their next assignments.

2. Tom is to focus on the _____ who benefit from the Festival.

_____ organizers   _____ people

_____ factories

3. Why did Lance call the Festival's organizers "the heart of our community"? _____

_____

Number of Words
Read per Minute

4. Check two sentences that are true. (2)

_____ The name of the school paper is *The Knightly News.*

_____ Betsy is a reporter for the paper.

_____ Unemployment is running high.

5. Check the main idea of the story.

_____ taking good photographs

_____ covering the Fall Festival

_____ Tom's writing talent

6. Why was Tom surprised when Ms. Lopez praised his work? _____

_____

7. Many people in Kendall are without work because _____ .

1. The Sierra Nevada lies _____ of San Francisco.

_____ east   _____ south   _____ north

2. Check the sentences that are true. (2)

_____ Ms. Lopez went mountain climbing at Yosemite National Park.

_____ Kim took photos of the scenery.

_____ The mountain air was warm.

_____ Ann got lost in the mountains.

3. Why were the tracks of the climbers' snowshoes the only marks in the snow?

_____

_____

Number of Words
Read per Minute

4. Check the main idea of the story.

_____ camping in the mountains

_____ writing about mountain climbing

_____ the importance of good snowshoes

5. Mountain climbers wear showshoes to _____ .

6. It was a challenge to climb the mountain because _____ .

7. Why might the mountain's snowy ground be dangerous? _____

_____

Test Score
(Possible Score — 8)

Checking Understanding

Test 3 These exercises are to be completed after reading the story on page 42.

1. Number the events in the order in which they happened in the story.

   ____ The class met at *The Kendall Bulletin.*

   ____ Mr. Martinez led the students to the newsroom.

   ____ The students watched the typesetting machine.

   ____ The students visited the press room.

   ____ Layout sheets were fed into the camera.

2. Write the names of two *Bulletin* departments the students visited. (2)

   _____

   _____

Number of Words Read per Minute [   ]

3. Why does the make-up crew place each story on a layout sheet? _____

   _____

4. Check two sentences that are true. (2)

   ____ The *Bulletin* camera is small.

   ____ The make-up crew places each story on a layout sheet.

   ____ The *Bulletin* is folded and cut.

5. Check the main idea of the story.

   ____ interviewing a reporter

   ____ taking a class trip

   ____ watching the newspaper process

6. Why do you think Tom's class visited the *Bulletin*? _____

Test Score (Possible Score — 8) [   ]

Test 4 These exercises are to be completed after reading the story on page 62.

1. The study of stars is called ____.

   ____ geology   ____ astronomy

   ____ galaxy

2. Check two sentences that are true. (2)

   ____ The stars move.

   ____ The sun is a star.

   ____ Stars never explode.

3. Write two reasons the *Bulletin* prints a night-sky map. (2)

   _____

   _____

Number of Words Read per Minute [   ]

4. Check the main idea of this story.

   ____ astronomy books

   ____ space travel in future years

   ____ interesting facts about stars

5. Astronomers use large telescopes to ____.

   ____ see the brightest stars

   ____ study the most distant stars

6. Why don't astronomers know exactly how many stars exist? _____

Test Score (Possible Score — 8) [   ]

Page 3 (top half)

Write the words from the story that have the meanings below.

1. meeting to get information

   interview
   (Par. 1)

2. news writer

   journalist
   (Par. 2)

3. wake up

   rouse
   (Par. 7)

In each row below, circle the three words that belong together.

4. (reporter) bakery (editor) (photographer)
5. (morning) (dawn) night (sunrise)
6. (school) (study) breakfast (classes)

Apostrophes are used to form **possessives**, words that show ownership. For example, *Tom's radio* means "the radio owned by Tom." Write possessives to complete the phrases.

Uncle Max   principal   alarm clock

1. the ___alarm clock's___ loud buzzing

2. the ___principal's___ newly painted office

3. ___Uncle Max's___ electric typewriter

Use two words from each sentence below to form a compound word. Write the compound word in the blank.

4. The bud of a rose is a ___rosebud___.

5. Work done at home is ___homework___.

6. A walk near the side of a road is a

   ___sidewalk___.

1. For what newspaper does Uncle Max work?

   ___The Kendall Bulletin___

2. Check the words that describe Tom.
   ✓ ambitious   ___ lazy
   ___ unfriendly   ✓ enthusiastic

3. A **fact** is something that is known to be true. An **opinion** is what a person believes, but an opinion may or may not be true. Put **F** before the sentence that is a fact.
   _F_ Men and women can be reporters.
   ___ This is a good newspaper.

4. Do you think Tom will pass his driver's test? Give reasons for your answer. ___

   (Answers will vary.)

1. Imagine you wanted to know more about Uncle Max's job. Check the subjects you could look up in the encyclopedia.
   ___ trucks   ✓ editing
   ✓ newspapers   ___ cameras

2. Suppose you wanted to know more about driving a car. Check the subjects you would look up.
   ___ sunglasses   ✓ traffic signs
   ✓ traffic laws   ___ mountains

3. **Guide words** are the two words in dark print at the top of a dictionary page. Check the words that would appear on a dictionary page that had the guide words **interview-introduce**.
   ✓ into   ___ intruder
   ___ investigate   ✓ intestines

Write the words from the story that have the meanings below.

1. possibility

   prospect
   (Par. 12)

2. with an uneasy feeling

   anxiously
   (Par. 14)

3. stood for

   represented
   (Par. 14)

4. damp

   clammy
   (Par. 14)

In each row below, circle the three words that belong together.

5. (car) (gasoline) (truck) backpack
6. (test) (exam) football (study)
7. (driver) muffin (pilot) (guide)

An ending that is added to a word to change its meaning or part of speech is called a **suffix**. The suffix **-ist** means "someone who does something." For example, the word *geologist* is "someone who studies geology." Add **-ist** to each word below. Then use the new word in a sentence.

1. organ ___organist___

   (Sentences will vary.)

2. cartoon ___cartoonist___

   (Sentences will vary.)

The suffix **-ly** can be added to some words. For example, a person who talks in a loud way talks **loudly**. Find the word in paragraph 14 of the story that means "in an anxious way."

3. ___anxiously___

1. Check the main idea of the story.
   ___ waking up late
   ___ playing football
   ✓ Tom's driving test

Write the word that best completes each sentence.

2. Tom poured the ___milk___ into the glass that was sitting on the counter.
   bread   milk   ocean

3. We ___estimated___ that fifty people attended last week's football game.
   confided   released   estimated

4. Why is Tom worried about passing his diving test? ___

   (Answers will vary.)

5. Find one sentence the author wrote to show how busy Tom's day was.

   ___With that, he hurried out of the house___

   ___to catch his bus.___

   (Answers may vary.)

Look at the chart and answer the questions.

Deadlines	Reporter	Department
May 4	Jenny	News
May 10	Christy	Art
May 12	Tom	Sports

1. Each deadline is in the month of ___May___

2. Who is the reporter for the sports page? ___Tom___

3. Which reporter has the last deadline?
   ___Tom___

3

Page 7 (bottom half)

Write the words from the story that have the meanings below.

1. workers

   staff
   (Par. 1)

2. great liking for

   admiration
   (Par. 4)

3. people who play sports

   athletes
   (Par. 4)

4. understandingly

   sympathetically
   (Par. 9)

5. A **simile** is a figure of speech in which two unlike things are compared. Similes use the word *like* or *as*. For example, *as sly as a fox* is a simile. Write a simile to describe how Tom entered his mother's restaurant.

   (Answers will vary.)

To form the possessive of a plural word that ends in *s*, add only an apostrophe. An example is *the girls' books*. Fill in each blank with the possessive form of the word in parentheses.

1. The ___customers'___ lunch order was taken by the headwaiter. (customers)

2. The ___waiters'___ aprons were hung in the kitchen. (waiters)

3. The ___students'___ tests were marked by the next day. (students)

4. The ___reporters'___ stories were typed with word processors. (reporters)

Write the word that best completes each sentence.

1. The ___server___ handed the girls a menu before seating them at a table.
   reporter   server   teacher

2. The girl knew ___exactly___ where the birds' nest could be found.
   cowardly   exactly   awfully

3. Number the events to show the order in which they happened.
   _4_ Tom sees his mom at The Hideaway.
   _2_ Tom takes his driving test.
   _1_ Ms. Lopez praises Tom's story.
   _5_ Mrs. Ellis congratulates Tom.
   _3_ Mrs. Hopple drives Tom to The Hideaway.

4. Tom passed his math test because

   (Answers will vary.)

5. Find one sentence the author wrote to show how Tom felt after his busy day.

   ___Oh, I'm so excited, I can___

   ___hardly think. (Answers may vary.)___

Write the name of the reference source that would provide the information needed.

atlas   thesaurus   almanac

1. Where could Betsy look to find out how much rain fell last year? ___almanac___

2. Where could Tom look to discover the location of the Black Hills? ___atlas___

3. Where could Jill look to find a synonym for the word *carve*? ___thesaurus___

Write the words from the story that have the meanings below.

1. speaking to

   addressing
   (Par. 15)

2. copy of a newspaper or magazine

   issue
   (Par. 15)

3. work given out

   assignments
   (Par. 16)

Words with opposite meanings are called **antonyms.** Find an antonym in the story for each of these words.

4. frowning ___smiling___
   (Par. 1)

5. less ___more___
   (Par. 7)

6. ran ___strolled___
   (Par. 14)

7. all ___some___
   (Par. 17)

8. shouted ___whispered___
   (Par. 18)

The suffix **-able** means "able to." This suffix can be added to verbs to form adjectives. Form new words and write a sentence with each adjective.

1. break + able = ___breakable___

   (Sentences will vary.)

2. wash + able = ___washable___

   (Sentences will vary.)

3. manage + able = ___manageable___

   (Sentences will vary.)

Write the word that best completes each sentence.

1. The latest ___issue___ of the paper will be delivered in the morning.
   issue   picture   journalism

2. The quarterback threw the ___ball___ to the player in the end zone.
   light   story   ball

3. Where will Tom's football story appear in the paper? ___the front page___

4. Tom offered to give Betsy a ride whenever she needed it. Why? ___She can't take her___

   ___driver's test for eight months.___

   (Answers may vary.)

5. Check the words that describe Betsy.
   ✓ friendly   ✓ supportive
   ___ nosy   ___ lazy

6. Check the main idea of paragraph 15.
   ___ Tom's journalism class
   ✓ meeting the deadline
   ___ new assignments for the next issue

The word you look up in a dictionary is called an **entry word**. All entry words are printed alphabetically in dark print down the left side of each column. Usually, an entry word is a base word. So if you want to know the meaning of *cities*, look for its base word, *city*. Next to each word below, write the entry word you would look for in the dictionary.

1. happier ___happy___   3. liked ___like___

2. faster ___fast___   4. slipping ___slip___

7

9

Knowing the Words

Write the words from the story that have the meanings below.

1. of a person

   personal
   (Par. 3)

2. said suddenly

   blurted
   (Par. 4)

3. concentrate

   focus
   (Par. 10)

4. things to do

   activities
   (Par. 11)

5. Check the sentence in which *running* has the same meaning it does in paragraph 9.

   ____ Tracy saw the horse running through the wet field.

   ____ Beth was running the lawn mower.

   _√_ Club attendance was running low due to heavy snow.

Find an antonym (opposite) in the story for each of these words.

6. last ____ first
   (Par. 3)

7. worst ____ best
   (Par. 8)

8. low ____ high
   (Par. 9)

Working with Words

A **prefix** is a group of letters added to the beginning of a word to change its meaning. The prefix **mid-** can mean "the middle part." For example, the word *midnight* means "the middle of the night." Add **mid-** to the word below. Use the new word in a sentence.

stream ____ midstream

(Sentences will vary.)

Reading and Thinking

1. Tom's school newspaper is named

   The Knightly News

2. Tom and Betsy's next assignment is to cover the ____ Fall Festival.

3. Check the main idea of paragraph 14.

   ____ helping families in need

   _√_ photographing activities at the Festival

   ____ square dancing

4. Ms. Lopez praised Tom's work because

   he had done a good job

   (Answers will vary.)

Put **F** before the sentences that are facts. Put **O** before the sentences that are opinions.

5. _O_ Everyone wants to be a reporter on a school newspaper.

6. _O_ Photography is a fun hobby.

7. _F_ There are many ways to earn money for special causes.

8. Do you think many citizens of Kendall will attend the Fall Festival? Why or why not?

   _____

   (Answers will vary.)

Learning to Study

Beside each word below, write the entry word you would look for in the dictionary.

1. foxes ____ fox
2. walked ____ walk
3. hugged ____ hug
4. clearly ____ clear
5. steepest ____ steep
6. answered ____ answer

Knowing the Words

Write the words from the story that have the meanings below.

1. way of doing something

   method
   (Par. 4)

2. turn down

   reject
   (Par. 5)

3. receive help

   benefit
   (Par. 12)

4. What is the simile in paragraph 9?

   slowly sinking like a

   ship in the water

5. Circle the three words that belong together.

   (festival)   (parade)

   cocoons   (games)

6. A **synonym** is a word with the same or nearly the same meaning as another word. Check the sets of words that are synonyms.

   _√_ ideas—thoughts

   _√_ now—immediately

   ____ day—night

   _√_ like—enjoy

Working with Words

Rewrite each group of words below. Use possessive forms.

1. the story belonging to Tom

   Tom's story

2. the cameras belonging to the men

   men's cameras

Reading and Thinking

1. Number the events to show the order in which they happened.

   _5_ Ms. Lopez praises Betsy's photos.

   _3_ Tom writes his story about the Festival.

   _2_ Tom and Betsy attend the Festival.

   _4_ Betsy goes to Tom's home.

   _1_ Tom and Betsy discuss their assignment.

2. Check each word or phrase that describes Ms. Lopez.

   ____ careless

   _√_ helpful

   _√_ expects the best from her students

3. Check two headlines that might have appeared in *The Knightly News* during the Fall Festival.

   ____ Flood Destroys Kendall

   _√_ Festival Parade Watched by 2,000

   _√_ Students Cover Fall Festival

4. Tom was very nervous when it was time to turn in his story. Find one sentence the author wrote to show how Tom felt.

   He felt his confidence slowly

   sinking like a ship in the water.

   (Answers may vary.)

Learning to Study

The signs below were used to help Kendall's visitors locate helpful services. Match the signs in the left column with the services they stand for in the right column.

1. _d_ ✚   a. Information
2. _e_ 🍴   b. Telephone
3. _a_ ❓   c. Baggage Check-In
4. _b_ 📞   d. First Aid
5. _c_ 🧳   e. Restaurant

Knowing the Words

Write the words from the story that have the meanings below.

1. praised

   complimented
   (Par. 1)

2. shy or uncomfortable feeling

   embarrassment
   (Par. 6)

3. in spite of

   despite
   (Par. 13)

4. Check the sentence in which *off* has the same meaning it does in paragraph 7.

   ____ Because I hadn't practiced for many weeks, my golf game was off.

   ____ Please turn off the lights when you finish.

   _√_ We all had some time off because the circus was in town.

Homophones are words that sound alike but have different meanings. Circle the homophone with the correct meaning in each sentence below.

5. Meg wants to go with Uncle Max (too,) two).

6. It took an (our, (hour) for the bus to arrive with the athletes.

Working with Words

The prefix **re-** means "again." The prefix **pre-** means "before." Read the clues. Add **re-** or **pre-** to each underlined word to form a word that matches the clue.

1. to <u>test</u> before ____ pretest

2. to <u>write</u> again ____ rewrite

3. to <u>paint</u> again ____ repaint

4. before a <u>game</u> ____ pregame

Reading and Thinking

1. Check the main idea of the story.

   ____ a great football game

   _√_ Tom's visit to the *Bulletin*

   ____ newspaper deadlines

2. A **summary** briefly expresses information about a topic. To summarize, you must find the most important information and put it in an order that makes sense. Read paragraph 13 from the story. Summarize the important information of the paragraph in one sentence.

   A newspaper office is busy

   around the clock. (Answers may vary.)

3. Why do you think the *Bulletin* reporters were working late at night?

   They were preparing for the

   Sunday edition. (Answers may vary.)

4. The *Bulletin* newsroom was very busy when Tom and Uncle Max arrived. Find one sentence the author wrote to show how busy it really was. Sure enough, the

   newsroom was bustling with noise

   when Tom and Uncle Max arrived.

   (Answers may vary.)

5. Do you think Tom will ever have another story printed in the *Bulletin*?

   Why or why not? ____ (Answers will vary.)

Learning to Study

A newspaper **caption** is a one- or two-sentence explanation of a newspaper photo. It usually appears under the photo. Write a caption for the photo of the football game.

_____

(Answers will vary.)

Knowing the Words

Write the words from the story that have the meanings below.

1. brags

   boasts
   (Par. 3)

2. statement made as a fact

   claim
   (Par. 3)

3. public attention

   publicity
   (Par. 6)

4. Check the phrase in which *slip* has the same meaning as it does in the newspaper headline in paragraph 3.

   ____ a small piece of paper

   ____ to lose balance

   _√_ to move quietly or easily

Working with Words

Rewrite each group of words below. Use possessive forms.

1. the handcuffs of the guards ____

   the guards' handcuffs

2. the escape of Houdini ____

   Houdini's escape

The prefix **ir-** usually means "not." Add **ir-** to each word below. Then use the new word in a sentence.

3. responsible ____ irresponsible

   (Sentences will vary.)

4. resistible ____ irresistible

   (Sentences will vary.)

5. regular ____ irregular

   (Sentences will vary.)

Reading and Thinking

1. Check the main idea of the story.

   ____ traveling around the world

   _√_ an amazing escape artist

   ____ how to perform magic tricks

2. What did people think of Houdini's acts before the front-page story?

   They didn't think Houdini's

   act was good.

3. How did the front-page story change Houdini's life? ____ It made

   him very popular.

   (Answers may vary.)

4. The author wrote this story to

   ____ talk about traveling.

   ____ explain Houdini's childhood.

   _√_ explain the effects of a newspaper story.

5. Write one change in Houdini's life after the newspaper story was printed. ____

   (Answers may vary.)

Learning to Study

Complete the following outline to explain what happened to Houdini in each place.

I. England

   A. Handcuffed and chained

   B. Tossed into a river

   C. Swam to the surface

II. Russia

   A. Locked in a cell

   B. Freed himself

Knowing the Words

Write the words from the story that have the meanings below.

1. gas, water, or electric service

   __utility__
   (Par. 6)

2. roller-shaped

   __cylinder__
   (Par. 7)

3. thick pieces of wood

   __beams__
   (Par. 7)

4. **Abbreviations** are shortened forms of words. Write this address without abbreviations.

   Dr. Trina Davis
   319 Oak St.
   New York, NY 10012

   __Doctor Trina Davis__

   __319 Oak Street__

   __New York, New York 10012__

Learning to Study

Complete this outline.
(Answers may vary.)

I. Things that were done before moving day

   A. __Obtained a permit__

   B. __Basement was dug__

   C. __Utilities disconnected__

   D. __Fragile objects removed__

II. Things that were done on moving day

   A. __House jacked up__

   B. __Beams put under the house__

   C. __House rolled to truck__

   D. __House put over new basement__

Reading and Thinking

1. Number of events to show the order in which they happened.

   __2__ A basement was dug for the house.

   __4__ The crew rolled the house to a flatbed truck using cylinders.

   __3__ The crew began to raise up the house using jacks.

   __1__ Mr. and Mrs. Davis obtained a permit.

   __5__ Betsy returned to class on Monday.

2. Why did Mr. and Mrs. Davis have to get a permit? __A permit was needed to transport a house on city streets.__

3. Why did the family have to remove from the house anything that was fragile? __The house-moving might have caused things to fall and break.__

4. Why was the house moved onto cylinder-shaped beams? __The beams could roll so the house could move more easily.__

5. The main idea of paragraph 8 is __the moving of the house__.

Working with Words

Sometimes suffixes are added to verbs to form nouns. Write the noun that is formed from each verb and suffix.

Verb	Suffix	Noun
1. depend	ence	dependence
2. correct	ion	correction
3. forgive	ness	forgiveness

19

Knowing the Words

Write the words from the story that have the meanings below.

1. lively

   __brisk__
   (Par. 1)

2. came to mind

   __occurred__
   (Par. 1)

3. stopping work for a special purpose

   __strike__
   (Par. 2)

4. a person you know

   __acquaintance__
   (Par. 13)

Find the synonym (word with similar meaning) in the story for each of these words.

5. part __section__
   (Par. 11)

6. film __movie__
   (Par. 11)

7. friend __acquaintance__
   (Par. 13)

Learning to Study

Read this newspaper coupon and answer the questions.

Lister's	One coupon
Limeade	per purchase
OFFER GOOD	
15¢ September 16–21 15¢	

1. If you used this newspaper coupon, how much money would you save? __15¢__

2. Could you use this coupon on September 30? Why or why not? __No. The coupon is good only until September 21.__

Reading and Thinking

1. The main idea of paragraph 9 is

   ___ entertainment in Fairlawn.

   _✓_ the strike's effects.

   ___ saving money.

2. The author wrote this story to

   ___ talk about strikes.

   ___ explain newspaper advertising.

   _✓_ explain the importance of a newspaper.

3. Write two effects the newspaper strike had on the people of Fairlawn.

   _____

   _____

   __(Answers will vary.)__

4. What might have happened if the strike had lasted longer than a month?

   _____

   _____

   __(Answers will vary.)__

Working with Words

Write the compound word from the list that makes sense in each sentence.

   footsteps   suitcases   sidewalk

1. Jean and I arrived at the airport without our __suitcases__.

2. As I was walking into the shop, I heard __footsteps__ behind me.

3. Shoppers had a hard time walking on the snow-covered __sidewalk__.

21

Knowing the Words

Write the words from the story that have the meanings below.

1. beautiful sights

   __scenery__
   (Par. 4)

2. exciting, thrilling

   __breathtaking__
   (Par. 4)

3. demanding

   __challenging__
   (Par. 5)

4. came down

   __descended__
   (Par. 11)

5. What is the simile in paragraph 7? __The mountain air was as cold as ice!__

Circle the word with the correct meaning in each sentence below.

6. May I have a (piece) peace) of watermelon?

7. Did you see the large (bear) bare) that stood near the foot of the mountain?

8. Carla likes to (read) reed) the newspaper when she wakes up in the morning.

Learning to Study

Entry words are divided into syllables. This shows where the words can be divided at the end of a line of writing. Divide these words into syllables.

1. val/ley
2. work/ing
3. moun/tain
4. si/lent
5. beau/ti/ful

6. news/pa/per
7. mus/cles
8. top/ics
9. sum/mer
10. col/lege

Reading and Thinking

Write the word that best completes each sentence.

1. Ann painted the __scenery__ yesterday.
   journey   sound   scenery

2. The goats __descended__ the cliff.
   propped   descended   suggested

3. How did the words *beautiful waterfall, silent forests,* and *deer grazing quietly* make you feel?

   ___ tired ___ upset _✓_ peaceful

4. Where is Yosemite National Park? __in the Sierra Nevadas__

5. Ms. Lopez and the others wore snowshoes because __they wanted to leave tracks in the snow__. __(Answers may vary.)__

6. Do you think Ms. Lopez will go mountain climbing again? Why or why not? __(Answers will vary.)__

Working with Words

The suffix **-ation** means "state, condition, action, or process of." For example, the word *presentation* means "the act of presenting." Add **-ation** to each word. Then use the new word in a sentence. You may have to drop the final *e* before adding the suffix.

1. expect __expectation__
   __(Sentences will vary.)__

2. imagine __imagination__
   __(Sentences will vary.)__

3. reserve __reservation__
   __(Sentences will vary.)__

23

Knowing the Words

Write the words from the story that have the meanings below.

1. unbelievable

   __incredible__
   (Par. 2)

2. meal in which diners serve themselves

   __buffet__
   (Par. 14)

3. crisp batter cakes

   __waffles__
   (Par. 14)

Check the three words in each column that belong together.

4. _✓_ band
   _✓_ parade
   _✓_ football game
   ___ science

5. _✓_ breakfast
   _✓_ juice
   ___ porch
   _✓_ pancakes

6. What is the simile in paragraph 2? __Tom came bounding down the stairs like a speeding locomotive.__

7. Check the sentence in which *planted* has the same meaning it does in paragraph 1.

   ___ Jean planted four rows of cucumbers.

   _✓_ Jo planted her feet in the dirt before swinging the bat.

Learning to Study

Complete the following outline.

I. Playing in a Band
   A. Playing well requires practice.
   B. _____ __(Answers will vary.)__

II. Choosing a Musical Instrument
   A. Some instruments are expensive.
   B. _____ __(Answers will vary.)__

Reading and Thinking

Write the word that best completes each sentence.

1. Melissa __opened__ a carton of milk.
   suggested   opened   crashed

2. The rain __splashed__ against the window, making it hard to see.
   splashed   talked   decided

3. In which section of the paper did Tom's story appear? __Community Interest__

4. Number the events to show the order in which they happened.

   __4__ Tom and his mom arrive at The Hideaway.

   __2__ Tom reads his story aloud.

   __5__ Customers arrive at the restaurant.

   __3__ Mrs. Ellis takes Meg to Kate's house.

   __1__ Tom wakes from sleeping.

5. The band members will be able to buy new uniforms because __the bake sale was a success__. __(Answers may vary.)__

Working with Words

The prefix **in-** sometimes means "not" or "the opposite of." Write words that have the following meanings by adding the prefix **in-** to a base word. Then use the new word in a sentence.

1. not correct __incorrect__
   __(Sentences may vary.)__

2. not direct __indirect__
   __(Sentences may vary.)__

25

Knowing the Words

Write the words from the story that have the meanings below.

2. contest between people or teams

competition
(Par. 7)

3. open building used for shelter

pavilion
(Par. 13)

4. main division of a country

province
(Par. 15)

Find antonyms (opposites) in the story for each of these words.

4. quickly ___slowly___
(Par. 1)

5. easy ___hard___
(Par. 3)

6. loosely ___tightly___
(Par. 6)

7. forget ___remember___
(Par. 14)

8. Write this address without abbreviations.

Mr. Luke Logan
261 Washington St.
Philadelphia, PA 19106

Mister Luke Logan

261 Washington Street

Philadelphia, Pennsylvania 19106

Working with Words

Fill in each blank with the possessive form of the word in parentheses.

1. The ___coach's___ new tennis racket was a gift from her students. (coach)

2. The ___athletes'___ awards were placed in the trophy case. (athletes)

3. My ___sister's___ coach flew to the track meet. (sister)

Reading and Thinking

1. Check the main idea of paragraph 13.
   ___ becoming a gymnast
   ___ a visit to Philadelphia
   ✓ the Liberty Bell

Put **F** before the sentences that are facts.
Put **O** before the sentences that are opinions.

2. _O_ Gymnastics is the most graceful sport.

3. _F_ The Liberty Bell weighs more than two thousand pounds.

4. _O_ Philadelphia is a great place.

5. Summarize the important information of paragraph 9 in one sentence.

   Meg must win first or second place

   in the competition to go to Philadelphia.
   (Answers may vary.)

6. Why did Meg rub her ankle after gymnastics practice? ___Because she'd fallen from the bar during practice.___

7. The author wrote this story to
   ✓ describe Philadelphia.
   ___ talk about gymnastics.
   ___ describe Meg's coach, Mr. Lee.

Learning to Study

Write the number of the encyclopedia volume that would have the most information for each of the topics below.

Vol. 1	Vol. 2	Vol. 3	Vol. 4	Vol. 5	Vol. 6	Vol. 7
A–C	D–F	G–J	K–M	N–Q	R–T	U–Z

1. The Liberty Bell ___4___

2. Independence Hall ___3___

3. The population of Pennsylvania ___5___

27

Knowing the Words

Write the words from the story that have the meanings below.

1. class

session
(Par. 3)

2. without full strength

gently
(Par. 11)

3. devotion

dedication
(Par. 16)

Match each word with its abbreviation.

4. _c_ Street   a. U.S.
5. _d_ Pennsylvania   b. Mr.
6. _a_ United States   c. St.
7. _b_ Mister   d. PA

Working with Words

Rewrite each group of words below. Use possessive forms.

1. the towel that is used by the gymnast
   ___gymnast's towel___

2. the covers of the books
   ___books' covers___

3. the game that belongs to Meg
   ___Meg's game___

4. the field that is used by the players
   ___players' field___

5. the green and white stripes of the flags
   ___flags' stripes___

6. the whistle that belongs to Tom
   ___Tom's whistle___

Reading and Thinking

1. How do you know Meg is determined to become a star athlete?
   _____
   (Answers will vary.)

2. Check the words that describe Mr. Lee.
   ✓ caring   ___ surprised
   ___ sad   ✓ wise

Put **F** before the sentences that are facts.
Put **O** before the sentences that are opinions.

3. _F_ A gymnast needs good balance.

4. _O_ Gymnastics is a difficult sport.

5. _F_ The balance beam is about four inches wide.

6. _O_ Gymnastics is the most graceful sport.

7. Do you think Meg will attend the competition in Philadelphia? Why or why not? _____
   _____
   (Answers will vary.)

Learning to Study

Complete this partial outline.

I. The Problems of Being a Gymnast
   A. Many hours of practice
   B. ___(Answers will vary.)___
   C. ___(Answers will vary.)___

Check the subjects you could look up in the encyclopedia if you wanted to know more about gymnastics.

✓ physical fitness   ✓ Olympic Games
___ racing   ___ tie-dyeing

29

Knowing the Words

Write the words from the story that have the meanings below.

1. in a certain neighborhood

local
(Par. 1)

2. life work

career
(Par. 3)

3. made-up story

fiction
(Par. 7)

4. reasonable opinions or decisions

conclusions
(Par. 8)

5. get hold of

capture
(Par. 12)

6. Write **S** between each pair of words that are synonyms, words with similar meanings.

professor	_S_	teacher
career	_S_	occupation
young	___	old
rising	___	falling
university	_S_	school

Learning to Study

You remember that entry words are divided into syllables. This shows where the words can be divided at the end of a line of writing. Divide the words below into syllables.

1. s c i/e n/t i s t
2. l i/b r a r y
3. c a/r e e r
4. i n/t e r/v i e w
5. a l/w a y s
6. e x/p e r/i/m e n t
7. f i c/t i o n
8. c a p/t u r e

Reading and Thinking

1. Check the main idea of the story.
   ___ the science fair
   ✓ an interesting interview
   ___ famous scientists

2. Check each word on phrase below that describes Dr. Stevens.
   ___ shy
   ___ lazy
   ✓ enjoys science
   ✓ helpful

Put **F** before the sentences that are facts.
Put **O** before the sentences that are opinions.

3. _F_ Experiments are done to test theories.

4. _O_ Science is the best subject.

5. _F_ People have stood on the moon.

6. Number the steps in the order they occur.
   _1_ A scientist develops an idea.
   _4_ Conclusions are drawn.
   _3_ Results of an experiment are studied.
   _2_ Experiments are done to test the idea.

Working with Words

Fill in each blank with the possessive form of the word in parentheses.

1. The ___sky's___ stars are countless. (sky)

2. The ___astronomer's___ book tells about the names of the stars. (astronomer)

3. The ___scientist's___ ideas were tested in the lab. (scientist)

31

Knowing the Words

Write the words from the story that have the meanings below.

1. not safe

endangered
(Par. 3)

2. process of dying out

extinction
(Par. 10)

3. something that makes the land, water, or air dirty

pollution
(Par. 12)

4. people who guard wildlife

game wardens
(Par. 14)

5. Check the sentence in which *light* has the same meaning as it does in paragraph 9.
   ___ The light flickered mysteriously before going completely out.
   ___ The newspaper carrier delivers papers before it is light out.
   ✓ A light rain covered the grass.

Working with Words

Use two words from each sentence to form a compound word, and write the new word in the blank.

1. A bird that is blue is a
   ___bluebird___

2. A cloth that covers a table is a
   ___tablecloth___

3. A shell that can be located near the sea is a ___seashell___

4. Wood that is used for building a fire is
   ___firewood___

Reading and Thinking

1. Check the main idea of the story.
   ___ going camping
   ✓ protecting wildlife
   ___ working as a game warden

2. Put a **C** before the phrases that tell what you might observe in a city, and put an **F** before the phrases that tell what you might observe in a forest.
   _F_ deer grazing
   _C_ traffic moving
   _C_ people shopping
   _F_ people hunting and fishing

3. Why must a game warden check to see that all is well in the forest? ___Some people do not obey hunting laws.___
   (Answers may vary.)

4. Write something Tom learned while camping with Uncle Max. _____
   (Answers will vary.)

5. Will the people who read Uncle Max's article respect wildlife more? Why or why not? _____
   _____
   (Answers will vary.)

Learning to Study

Check the words that would appear on a dictionary page having these guide words.

babies—backward
✓ baboon
✓ bachelor
___ bark
✓ back
✓ backward

icing—illness
___ imitate
✓ idol
✓ ideal
___ icecap
✓ ignore

33

Knowing the Words

Write the words from the story that have the meanings below.

1. very or unbelievably
   <u>incredibly</u>
   (Par. 1)

2. making a short, snapping sound
   <u>clicking</u>
   (Par. 12)

3. very great
   <u>tremendous</u>
   (Par. 12)

4. understand clearly
   <u>realize</u>
   (Par. 14)

5. done by hand
   <u>manual</u>
   (Par. 16)

In each row below, circle the three words that belong together.

6. (rain) (thunder) heat (lightning)
7. (city) river (town) (village)
8. (summer) (sun) (beach) snow
9. (college) (school) (study) map
10. discuss (halt) (pause) (stop)

Learning to Study

A **pronunciation key** is a list of sound symbols and key words. They tell how to pronounce dictionary entry words. Use the pronunciation key on the inside back cover of this book to write the words that match these respellings.

1. /nūz′ pā′ pər/   <u>newspaper</u>
2. /ärt′ i kəl/   <u>article</u>
3. /wən(t)s/   <u>once</u>
4. /hȯlt/   <u>halt</u>

Reading and Thinking

Write the word that best completes each sentence.

1. The <u>rain</u> poured through the hole in the barn's roof.
   newspaper   rain   exactly

2. Everyone read the good news in the newspaper's <u>headline</u>.
   headline   company   editors

3. How was *The Times* different after the storm knocked out the electricity?
   <u>The presses stopped and editors</u>
   <u>used manual typewriters.</u>

4. The main idea of paragraph 16 is
   ✓ the effects of the thunderstorm.
   ___ preparing the paper for printing.
   ___ Ms. Lopez's job at *The Times*.

5. When Ms. Lopez worked at *The Times*, she lived in <u>Mill Creek</u>

6. Write one phrase the author used to describe the mood or feeling in the newsroom after the power went out.
   <u>Then, everything was still.</u>

Working with Words

Fill in each blank with the possessive form of the word in parentheses.

1. The <u>thunder's</u> noise frightened the small child. (thunder)

2. The <u>newspaper's</u> presses stopped after a flash of lightning. (newspaper)

3. When the lights went out, Linda discovered that the <u>flashlight's</u> batteries were dead. (flashlight)

Knowing the Words

Write the words from the story that have the meanings below.

1. people who study plants and animals
   <u>biologists</u>
   (Par. 5)

2. freight carried by a ship
   <u>cargo</u>
   (Par. 7)

3. a thickness or fold
   <u>layer</u>
   (Par. 11)

4. Write **A** between each pair of words that are antonyms, words with opposite meanings.
   sea   <u>A</u>   land
   sink   <u>A</u>   float
   dive   ___   plunge

Match each word with its abbreviation.

5. <u>b</u> pounds   a. NM
6. <u>c</u> Florida   b. lbs.
7. <u>a</u> New Mexico   c. FL

Learning to Study

Read this weather report. Then answer the questions below.

> **Tarpon Times Weather**
> –Partly cloudy, warm tonight and Friday
> –Low tonight around 60 degrees
> –High Friday in the 80s

1. Will there be heavy rainstorms during the night? <u>no</u>

2. The lowest temperature on Thursday night will be about <u>60</u>

Reading and Thinking

Write the word that best completes each sentence.

1. I am interested in studying about <u>marine</u> anim___
   marine   certainly   helmet

2. The gift was not <u>expensive</u>
   various   main   expensive

3. What does Ana gather from the Gulf o___ Mexico? <u>sponges</u>

4. Check two sentences that are true.
   ✓ Divers are warmly dressed.
   ✓ A diver's clothes are expensive.
   ___ All divers are marine biologists.

5. The author wrote this story to
   ___ describe Tarpon Springs, Florida.
   ___ explain marine biology.
   ✓ inform readers about diving.

6. Ana knows a great deal about diving equipment because
   <u>(Answers will vary.)</u>

Working with Words

Rewrite each group of words below. Use possessive forms.

1. shoes of the diver <u>diver's shoes</u>
2. members of the team <u>team's member___</u>
3. tools of the crew <u>crew's tools</u>
4. suit that belongs to Ana <u>Ana's</u>
5. cargo of the ship <u>ship's cargo</u>
6. floor of the ocean <u>ocean's floor</u>
7. story written by Max <u>Max's story</u>

Knowing the Words

Write the words from the story that have the meanings below.

1. became more gentle
   <u>mellowed</u>
   (Par. 2)

2. spoke with stops and starts
   <u>stammered</u>
   (Par. 9)

3. really
   <u>actually</u>
   (Par. 13)

4. What is the simile in paragraph 10?
   <u>Max was as eager as a beaver.</u>

5. Circle the three words that belong together.
   (friend)   enemy
   (acquaintance)   (playmate)

Learning to Study

In each blank, write the name of the correct reference book.

atlas   thesaurus   almanac

1. Where could you look to find out how many miles Tarpon Springs is from Cape Canaveral? <u>atlas</u>

2. Where could you look to find out some of the major events of 1997? <u>almanac</u>

3. Where could you find a synonym for *research*? <u>thesaurus</u>

4. Where could you look to find the name of the governor of Florida? <u>almanac</u>

Reading and Thinking

Write the word that best completes each sentence.

1. Lynn was <u>eager</u> to begin her art lessons.
   suspicious   eager   lazy

2. Jeff <u>introduced</u> the reporter to his class.
   introduced   laughed   rejected

3. The main idea of paragraph 13 is
   ___ being an accountant.
   ✓ the importance of checking the facts.
   ___ working for a large corporation.

4. Max's story did not appear in the paper because <u>he failed to check</u> <u>his facts</u>.
   (Answers may vary.)

5. How did Uncle Max's reporting style change after his story was pulled from the paper?
   <u>Uncle Max remembered to check all facts.</u>

Working with Words

These nouns have base words that are verbs. Fill in the chart.

Noun	Verb	Suffix
1. rotation	rotate	ion
2. assignment	assign	ment
3. adoption	adopt	ion
4. objection	object	ion
5. replacement	replace	ment
6. imagination	imagine	ation
7. payment	pay	ment

Knowing the Words

Write the words from the story that have the meanings below.

1. appeared in print
   <u>published</u>
   (Par. 3)

2. central part
   <u>core</u>
   (Par. 5)

3. give out
   <u>assign</u>
   (Par. 7)

4. accepts or gives permission for
   <u>approves</u>
   (Par. 11)

Circle the word with the correct meaning in each sentence below.

5. I (know) no) where the bank is located.
6. We brought (our) hour) lunches with us when we attended the concert.
7. The girls placed (they're (their) shoes in the trunk.
8. What are you going to (where, (wear) to the festival?

Working with Words

The suffixes **-hood** and **-ship** usually mean "the state or condition of being." Add **-hood** and **-ship** to each word below. Then use the new word in a sentence.

1. child <u>childhood</u>
   (Sentences will vary.)

2. leader <u>leadership</u>
   (Sentences will vary.)

3. neighbor <u>neighborhood</u>
   (Sentences will vary.)

Reading and Thinking

1. Number the events in the order in whi___ they happen.
   <u>5</u> The dummy sheet is approved by the managing editor.
   <u>1</u> The city editor assigns each story to a reporter.
   <u>4</u> The copy editor types a headlin___ the story.
   <u>3</u> The copy editor checks the facts i___ the story.
   <u>2</u> The reporter investigates and writ___ the story.

Put **F** before the sentences that are facts. Put **O** before the sentences that are opinions.

2. <u>O</u> The reporters have the most important job at the paper.
3. <u>F</u> A city editor gives each story to a reporter.
4. <u>O</u> The copy editor's job is the hardes___
5. <u>F</u> The dummy sheets show where each item in the paper will go.
6. <u>F</u> A photographer often accompanie___ the reporter.
7. The author wrote this story to
   ___ invite people to a newspaper firm.
   ✓ tell about the newspaper business.
   ___ describe Jim Martinez's job.

Learning to Study

Check the reference source you might use ___ find out more about newspaper publishing

___ an atlas
✓ an encyclopedia
___ a dictionary
___ a thesaurus

Knowing the Words

Write the words from the story that have the meanings below.

1. setting the words into type

   typesetting
   (Par. 4)

2. setting up type

   composing
   (Par. 5)

3. pushed lightly

   nudged
   (Par. 7)

4. Check the sentence in which *sheet* has the same meaning as it does in paragraph 5.

   ___ Barb put a clean sheet on the bed.

   _✓_ Ms. Lopez handed me the answer sheet after I sharpened my pencil.

   ___ Meg washed the cookie sheet after she finished baking.

Learning to Study

Look at the time line and answer the questions below.

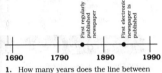

1690   1790   1890   1990

1. How many years does the line between each pair of dates stand for? **100**

2. Which of the two events on the time line occurred first? **the first regularly published newspaper**

3. Would the year 2090 be on the right or left side of the time line? **right**

Reading and Thinking

Write the word that best completes each sentence.

1. The headline was **typed** into the computer.

   written   typed   addressed

2. Mr. Martinez **led** the students into the composing room.

   refused   run   led

3. Who writes the story's headline?

   the copy editor

4. Who prepares the layout sheet?

   the make-up crew

5. Why did Tom think Betsy would be excited to see the *Bulletin's* camera?

   (Answers will vary.)

6. Do you think Tom will work at the *Bulletin* someday? Give reasons for your answer.

   (Answers will vary.)

Working with Words

Use two words from each sentence to form a compound word, and write the compound word in the blank.

1. A coat worn in the rain is a **raincoat**.

2. A tie that is worn around the neck is a

   necktie.

3. A brush that is used for cleaning each

   tooth is a **toothbrush**.

4. A ball that is thrown through a basket

   is a **basketball**.

43

Knowing the Words

Write the words from the story that have the meanings below.

1. yearly celebration

   anniversary
   (Par. 1)

2. old-fashioned

   outdated
   (Par. 7)

Find a synonym (word with similar meaning) in the story for each of these words.

3. story **article**
   (Par. 1)

4. concentrate **focus**
   (Par. 2)

5. quicker **faster**
   (Par. 5)

6. cellar **basement**
   (Par. 6)

7. assistance **help**
   (Par. 13)

Learning to Study

Read the dictionary entries and answer the questions below.

¹**type** /tɪp/ *n* **1** a class or group having common characteristics **2** printed or typewritten letters

²**type** *v* to write with a typewriter

1. In which entry is *type* a noun?

   first entry

2. In which entry is *type* a verb?

   second entry

3. How many syllables does *type* have? **1**

4. Look at entry ¹**type**. Which definition gives the meaning of *type* as it is used in paragraph 4? **1**

Reading and Thinking

1. Number the events in the order in which they happen.

   _1_ The Linotype operator types each line.

   _4_ The lead blocks are coated with ink.

   _5_ The newspaper is printed page by page.

   _2_ The lead inside the Linotype machine heats up.

   _3_ The blocks of letters are fitted together.

2. Write one way the *Bulletin* newsroom is different now than when the newspaper was first founded.

   (Answers will vary.)

Write the word that best completes each sentence.

3. Air **pollution** can be a problem in a large city.

   deadlines   keyboards   pollution

4. Meg spoke **excitedly** about the new bike.

   furiously   excitedly   friendly

Working with Words

Rewrite each group of words below. Use possessive forms.

1. the wings of the birds

   birds' wings

2. the tail of the monkey

   monkey's tail

3. the game that belongs to Kim

   Kim's game

45

Knowing the Words

Write the words from the story that have the meanings below.

1. with strength

   forcefully
   (Par. 4)

2. method

   technique
   (Par. 6)

3. warming up

   limbering up
   (Par. 6)

4. What is the simile in paragraph 10?

   something that hit him like a ton of bricks

Working with Words

The prefix **un-** means "not" or "the opposite of." For example, the word *unlock* means "the opposite of lock," while the word *unsafe* means "not safe." Add **un-** to each of the words, and write the new words in the blanks.

   happy   tie

1. Denise began to **untie** the twisted knot in her shoestring.

2. The small child looked **unhappy** as she watched the balloon float away.

The prefix **dis-** can also mean "not" or "the opposite of." Write words that have the following meanings by adding the prefix **dis-** to a base word. Then use the new word in a sentence.

3. not like **dislike**

   (Sentences will vary.)

4. the opposite of connect **disconnect**

   (Sentences will vary.)

Reading and Thinking

1. Check the main idea of the story.

   ___ running on the track team

   _✓_ a forgotten meeting

   ___ becoming a track star

2. Tom will be late for his interview with the mayor because **he forgot the appointment**

3. How do you think the mayor will react once Tom arrives for the interview?

   (Answers will vary.)

4. Describe the kind of person Coach Palmer is. **(Answers will vary.)**

Learning to Study

This is part of an application. It is the paper that students must fill out when they want to join the track team. Read the application and answer the questions.

NAME			
	Last	First	Middle
ADDRESS			
	Number		Street
	City	State	ZIP
BIRTH DATE			
	Day	Month	Year

1. What part of the name is written last?

   middle name

2. What part of the application tells the person's age? **birth date**

3. What should be written first on the address line? **number**

47

Knowing the Words

Write the words from the story that have the meanings below.

1. ran at full speed

   sprinted
   (Par. 2)

2. became red suddenly

   flushed
   (Par. 6)

3. person who is treated badly

   victim
   (Par. 9)

Circle the word with the correct meaning in each sentence below.

4. Because the crowd was in her (way) weigh), Beth couldn't cross the street.

5. Do you know (wear, (where) my running shoes are?

6. Please (pour) poor) the water into the bigger glass.

Find a synonym (word with similar meaning) in the story for each of these words.

7. worry **anxiety**
   (Par. 1)

8. article **story**
   (Par. 7)

Learning to Study

Use the pronunciation key on the inside back cover of this book to write the words that match these respellings.

1. /vik´ təm/ **victim**

2. /ang zī´ət ē/ **anxiety**

3. /ȯf´ əs/ **office**

4. /fīn´ əl ē/ **finally**

5. /mā´ ər/ **mayor**

Reading and Thinking

Write the word that best completes each sentence.

1. Jenny **slammed** the door as she hurried to catch the bus.

   slammed   poked   started

2. The tall **building** is at the corner of First and Third Streets.

   mayor   building   desk

3. The mayor's **speech** was heard by hundreds of citizens.

   office   speech   raincoat

4. What time was Tom's appointment to interview the mayor? **four o'clock**

5. What did Tom decide to write his article about? **being forgetful**

6. Tom wasn't able to interview the mayor because **he arrived too late**.

7. Do you think Tom will remember important appointments from now on?

   Give reasons for your answer. **(Answers will vary.)**

Working with Words

Use a word from row A and a word from row B to form a compound word to complete each sentence. The word you form must make sense in the sentence.

A. book   bed   any
B. one   case   room

1. Has **anyone** seen my notebook?

2. I think I left it in my **bedroom**.

3. Please look on the top shelf of my **bookcase**.

49

Knowing the Words

Write the words from the story that have the meanings below.

1. motions used to express ideas

   __gestures__
   (Par. 3)

2. not able to hear fully

   __hearing impaired__
   (Par. 3)

3. express ideas and thoughts

   __communicate__
   (Par. 5)

4. using gestures to speak

   __signing__
   (Par. 12)

5. Check the sentence in which *drew* has the same meaning as it does in paragraph 12.

   ___ Sharon drew a beautiful picture of daffodils.

   _✓_ We drew nearer to the warmth of the campfire.

   ___ He drew the wrong conclusion from the facts that were presented.

Working with Words

The prefix **fore-** means "front" or "before." For example, the word *forearm* means "the front of the arm." Add **fore-** to each word. Then use the new word in a sentence.

1. head ___forehead___

   (Sentences will vary.)

2. cast ___forecast___

   (Sentences will vary.)

3. told ___foretold___

   (Sentences will vary.)

Reading and Thinking

1. *Ameslan* is another word for

   __American Sign Language__

2. Where did Laurent Clerc teach French Sign Language? __Paris__

3. Why did Dr. Hayman tell Tom he would learn more from a personal interview?

   __Tom would see sign language__
   __actually being used.__

4. The author wrote this story to

   ___ invite readers to visit the Beam School.

   ___ explain hearing impairments.

   _✓_ inform readers about American Sign Language.

5. Write a fact Tom learned about American Sign Language.

   __(Answers will vary.)__

6. Write an opinion that Tom may have formed after his trip to the Beam School for the Deaf. ___

   __(Answers will vary.)__

Learning to Study

Complete this outline.

I. The History of American Sign Language

   A. __Based on French Sign Language__

   B. __Not accepted until the 1960s__

II. Using American Sign Language

   A. __Shape of the hand__

   B. __Position of hand next to body__

51

Knowing the Words

Write the words from the story that have the meanings below.

1. very old furniture and accessories

   __antique__
   (Par. 3)

2. people who buy and sell

   __dealers__
   (Par. 6)

3. items for sale

   __wares__
   (Par. 6)

4. something extra

   __bonus__
   (Par. 6)

In each row below, circle the three words that belong together.

5. (couch) (chair) grass (table)

6. (dealer) story (merchant) (wares)

7. (China) Florida (Japan) (Asia)

8. (walnut) (oak) (pine) sand

Circle the word with the correct meaning in each sentence below.

9. Shopping for antiques is (your, you're) favorite way to relax.

10. Did you (buy, by) any antiques today?

Working with Words

Fill in each blank with the possessive form of the word in parenthesis.

1. The ___dealers'___ wares were on display. (dealers)

2. The ___antiques'___ prices were marked on small cards. (antiques)

3. ___Diane's___ notes were left on the table. (Diane)

Reading and Thinking

Write the word that best completes each sentence.

1. Antique collecting is a ___popular___ hobby.

   level   broken   popular

2. The ___merchant___ is planning furniture sale.

   merchant   lumber   portrait

3. How old must an item be before it is considered an antique? __100 years old__

4. What was the purpose of a wing chair?

   __A wing chair protected a person__
   __from drafts.__

Put **F** before the sentences that are facts. Put **O** before the sentences that are opinions.

5. _O_ Everyone likes collecting antiques.

6. _O_ The best antiques are found in small antique shops.

7. _F_ If an item is old enough and charming enough, it can become an antique.

8. _F_ Some people collect antique cars.

Learning to Study

Read the dictionary entry below. Then answer the questions.

wing / wing / *n* **1** one of the movable parts of a bird or insect used in flying **2** part that sticks out from the main part or body

1. What part of speech is *wing*? __noun__

2. Which definition gives the meaning of *wing* as it is used in paragraph 13? _

5

Knowing the Words

Write the words from the story that have the meanings below.

1. sound

   __tone__
   (Par. 3)

2. teach

   __tutor__
   (Par. 5)

3. puts in

   __inserts__
   (Par. 7)

Find an antonym (word that has opposite meaning) in the story for each of these words.

4. departed ___arrived___
   (Par. 1)

5. seldom ___often___
   (Par. 10)

Learning to Study

Look at the map and answer the questions below.

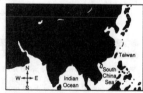

1. Which island country is southeast of China? ___Taiwan___

2. Which body of water is southwest of Taiwan? ___South China Sea___

3. Which body of water is south of India? ___Indian Ocean___

Reading and Thinking

1. What is the name of the port city that Kwan Lee comes from? __Jiangmen__

2. What jobs do Kwan's father and mother have? __doctor and teacher__

3. From the story, write one way that China and the United States are alike.

   ___
   __(Answers will vary.)__

4. From the story, write one way that China and the United States are different.

   ___
   __(Answers will vary.)__

5. Summarize the important information of paragraph 10 in one sentence.

   __In China, a rest period occurs__
   __every afternoon. (Answers may vary.)__

6. The author wrote this story to

   ___ explain how to cook in a wok.

   ___ talk about traveling.

   _✓_ describe life in China.

Working with Words

The suffix **-ment** often means "the state or condition of being." For example, the word *retirement* means "the state or condition of being retired." Write a word to match each definition below. Then write a sentence using each word.

1. the state of being improved __improvement__

   (Sentences will vary.)

2. the state of being excited __excitement__

   (Sentences will vary.)

55

Knowing the Words

Write the words from the story that have the meanings below.

1. television broadcast room

   __studio__
   (Par. 8)

2. things built by human hands

   __structure__
   (Par. 14)

3. stop or do away with

   __cancel__
   (Par. 15)

Find a synonym (word with similar meaning) in the story for each of these words.

4. broadcaster ___announcer___
   (Par. 4)

5. positions ___places___
   (Par. 8)

6. concluded ___finished___
   (Par. 18)

7. Check the three words that belong together.

   _✓_ newscast   _✓_ announcer
   _✓_ television   ___ apartment

Working with Words

The suffix **-ful** usually means "full of." For example, the word *helpful* means "full of help." Write a word to match each definition below. Then write a sentence using each word.

1. full of wonder ___wonderful___

   (Sentences will vary.)

2. full of cheer ___cheerful___

   (Sentences will vary.)

3. full of care ___careful___

   (Sentences will vary.)

Reading and Thinking

1. Number the events to show the order in which they happened.

   _5_ Tom announces the weather.

   _1_ Ms. Lopez suggested a televised news journal.

   _2_ Susan tells Ms. Lopez that she's nervous about doing the show.

   _4_ Tom tells the day's menu.

   _3_ Betsy aims her camera.

2. Check the words that describe Tom at the beginning of the story.

   _✓_ nervous   ___ happy
   ___ relaxed   _✓_ anxious

3. Tom tried out to be an announcer because ___

   __(Answers will vary.)__

Learning to Study

Write the name of the reference source that would provide the information needed.

   dictionary   Biographical Dictionary
   thesaurus   encyclopedia

1. Where could Julie look to find out when news reporter Walter Cronkite was born?

   __Biographical Dictionary__

2. Where could Tim look to find a synonym for the word *broadcast*? __thesaurus__

3. Where could you look to find an article about sportscasting? __encyclopedia__

4. Where could Rita look to find the meaning of the word *studio*? __dictionary__

5

Knowing the Words

Write the words from the story that have the meanings below.

1. chemically made material that can be shaped

   __plastic__
   (Par. 3)

2. unusually small

   __midget__
   (Par. 4)

3. different kinds

   __varieties__
   (Par. 4)

Learning to Study

A circle graph is a chart that shows how something is divided into its different parts. This circle graph shows the percentage sold of four popular flowers that Tom saw at the Flower Show. Read the circle graph. Answer the questions below it.

daisy 50%
tulip 35%
daffodil 8%
iris 7%

1. Which flower was the most popular?

   __daisy__

2. Which flower was least popular? __iris__

3. Which flower had thirty-five percent of the total sales? __tulip__

4. Which flower was third in popularity?

   __daffodil__

Reading and Thinking

Write the word that best completes each sentence.

1. Jan used all her __energy__ planting her vegetable garden.

   appreciation   panic   energy

2. The plastic sheet offered __shelter__ for the newly planted seeds.

   shelter   funnel   humid

3. Check the main idea of the story.

   ___ a flower show

   ___ growing African violets

   _✓_ planting a bag garden

4. Why didn't Tom want to plant the seeds outside? __Frost might harm the__ __seedlings.__

5. Do you think Meg's bag garden will grow? Why or why not? _____

   (Answers will vary.)

Working with Words

You remember that the prefix pre- means "before." Add pre- to each word and write the meaning of the word.

1. pay __prepay__

   to pay before

2. view __preview__

   to see before

3. historic __prehistoric__

   before written history

4. heat __preheat__

   to heat before

59

Knowing the Words

Write the words from the story that have the meanings below.

1. of the moon

   __lunar__
   (Par. 2)

2. darkness of the sun or moon

   __eclipse__
   (Par. 2)

3. of the sun

   __solar__
   (Par. 4)

4. shades of color

   __hues__
   (Par. 12)

Learning to Study

This chart shows the countries where some total solar eclipses were seen or will be seen. Read the chart and answer the questions.

	Seen from Eastern Hemisphere	Seen from Western Hemisphere
March 18, 1988	Borneo, Philippines	
July 22, 1990	Finland	
Oct. 24, 1995	Iran	
Feb. 26, 1998		Colombia, Venezuela
Aug. 11, 1999	India	

1. The eclipse that will occur on August 11, 1999 will be seen from the __Eastern__ Hemisphere.

2. Write the names of the countries from which an eclipse was seen on March 18, 1988. __Borneo, Philippines__

3. An eclipse was seen from Finland. What was the date on which it happened?

   __July 22, 1990__

Reading and Thinking

Complete each sentence with the correct word or words from the story.

1. Earth __orbits__ the sun.

2. A solar eclipse happens when the moon goes between the __earth__ and the __sun__.

3. Check the main idea of the story.

   ___ learning about the earth's atmosphere

   _✓_ learning about eclipses

   ___ photographing an eclipse

4. Put F before the sentences that are facts. Put O before the sentences that are opinions.

   _F_ Solar eclipses are more common than lunar eclipses.

   _O_ A solar eclipse is nature's best show.

   _F_ The moon orbits the earth.

   _O_ We should all watch an eclipse.

5. Read paragraph 2 from the story. Summarize the important information of the paragraph in one sentence.

   __A lunar eclipse occurs when the earth__ __comes between the sun and the moon.__

   (Answers may vary.)

Working with Words

Rewrite each group of words below. Use possessive forms.

1. the suit of the astronaut

   __astronaut's suit__

2. the shadow of the sun

   __sun's shadow__

61

Knowing the Words

Write the words from the story that have the meanings below.

1. energy made from split atoms

   __atomic energy__
   (Par. 4)

2. colorless gas that burns

   __hydrogen__
   (Par. 4)

3. one thousand million

   __billion__
   (Par. 6)

4. Write a simile to describe the appearance of the stars in the sky. Remember to use like or as in your description.

   _____
   (Answers will vary.)

In each row below, circle the three words that belong together.

5. (sun) (stars) grass (moon)

6. (galaxy) (Saturn) (Milky Way) boat

7. (month) (day) (year) east

Learning to Study

Complete the following outline.

I. The life of the stars

   A. Begin in a cloud of gas and dust

   B. Shine because of hydrogen

   C. Explode at loss of hydrogen

II. The motion of the stars

   A. Seem to rise in the east

   B. Seem to set in the west

   C. Spin around the galaxy's center

Reading and Thinking

1. Where does a star begin? __inside__ __a cloud__

2. What is needed to make atomic energy?

   __hydrogen__

3. Our galaxy is known as __the Milky Way__.

4. The main idea of paragraph 4 is

   ___ telescopes.

   _✓_ the life of a star.

   ___ the Milky Way.

5. Long ago people observed the night sky to tell time. How did the movement of the stars show the time of night?

   __The movement of the stars from east__ __to west showed the time of night.__

6. Uncle Max knew a great deal about the stars because _____

   (Answers will vary.)

Working with Words

You remember that the suffix -ation means "state, condition, action, or process of." Add -ation to each word. Then use the new word in a sentence. You may have to drop the final e before you add the suffix.

1. reserve __reservation__

   (Sentences will vary.)

2. accuse __accusation__

   (Sentences will vary.)

3. The suffix -ion can mean "state, condition, action, or process of." What does the word addition mean?

   __the act of adding__

63

Knowing the Words

Write the words from the story that have the meanings below.

1. a large, round roof or ceiling

   __dome__
   (Par. 4)

2. highest rank

   __supreme__
   (Par. 7)

3. a judge

   __justice__
   (Par. 10)

4. place where people are buried

   __cemetery__
   (Par. 11)

5. What abbreviation in the story stands for District of Columbia? __D.C.__

6. What is the abbreviation for United States? __U.S.__

Learning to Study

Here is a copy of Tom's airline ticket. Read it and answer the questions.

```
SUN AIRLINES
Name of Passenger
Tom Ellis
                    Flight    Date    Time
From: Kendall       406       4/17    6:00 P.M.
Arriving: Washington, D.C.    4/17    9:00 P.M.
Ticket Number:   005 321 685
```

1. What time will Tom leave Kendall?

   __6:00 P.M.__

2. On what date will he fly? __4/17__

3. On what airline will Tom fly?

   __Sun Airlines__

Reading and Thinking

1. How many rooms are in the Capitol?

   __540__

2. Who planned the city of Washington, D.C.?

   __Major Pierre Charles L'Enfant__

3. Washington, D.C., covers how many square miles? __69__

4. Put B before the phrases that describe Washington before it was finished. Put A before the phrases that describe the city after it was finished.

   _B_ muddy, torn up ground

   _B_ no paved streets

   _B_ half-finished government offices

   _A_ trees and gardens on the White House grounds

5. Write one fact Tom learned about the Capitol. _____

   (Answers will vary.)

6. Write an opinion that Tom may have formed after visiting the Capitol.

   _____
   (Answers will vary.)

Working with Words

After reading each sentence, write the compound word that correctly fills each blank.

1. Meg packed a __suitcase__ before she left for vacation. (suitcase, mailbox)

2. We arrived at the __airport__ just as the plane took off. (sidewalk, airport)

3. Has __anyone__ seen my airline ticket? (everywhere, anyone)

65

Knowing the Words

Write the words from the story that have the meanings below.

1. a type of glass

   crystal
   (Par. 4)

2. visitors

   tourists
   (Par. 7)

3. in a special manner

   specially
   (Par. 10)

4. way something looks

   appearance
   (Par. 13)

5. What is the simile in paragraph 4?

   chandeliers that looked

   like frozen fountains

Learning to Study

Read the dictionary entry and answer the questions below.

pres i dent /prez′ə dənt/ *n* the chief officer of a company, college, club, or society

1. Would the word *press* come before or

   after *president*? _____ after

2. What part of speech is *president*?

   noun

3. Write the word *president* in syllables.

   pres i dent

4. Write two guide words that might appear on the dictionary page where *president* is found.

   (Answers will vary.)

Reading and Thinking

Put **T** before each sentence that is true. Put **F** before each sentence that is false.

1. __F__ Most photographs show the south side of the White House.

2. __T__ Crystal chandeliers hang in the East Room.

3. __F__ The Lincoln Room is located on the first floor.

4. __T__ The President and the President's family live on the third floor.

5. The main idea of paragraph 2 is

   a description of the outside

   of the White House
   (Answers will vary.)

Write the word that best completes each sentence.

6. You certainly are _____ entitled _____ to a long vacation.

   entitled   continued   concentrated

7. The group will _____ provide _____ a map to the White House.

   encourage   rescue   provide

8. Do you think Tom will visit the White House again? Why or why not?

   _____

   (Answers will vary.)

Working with Words

The suffix **-an** means "one who is from." For example, an American is someone "who is from America." Use **-an** to form a word that correctly completes each sentence.

1. One who is from Asia is _____ Asian _____.

2. One who is from Ohio is an _____ Ohioan _____.

3. One who is from Hawaii is a _____ Hawaiian _____.

67

Knowing the Words

Write the words from the story that have the meanings below.

1. special article

   feature
   (Par. 1)

2. dressed

   clad
   (Par. 4)

3. measurement of depth

   fathoms
   (Par. 5)

4. a bright, starlike heavenly body

   comet
   (Par. 10)

5. Write **A** between each pair of words that are antonyms, words with opposite meanings.

   always __A__ never
   friend __A__ enemy
   helper ____ assistant
   dull __A__ exciting
   clap ____ applaud

Learning to Study

Write the number of the encyclopedia volume that would have the most information for each of the topics below.

Vol. 1	Vol. 2	Vol. 3	Vol. 4	Vol. 5	Vol. 6	Vol. 7
A–C	D–F	G–J	K–M	N–Q	R–T	U–Z

1. Mississippi River __4__

2. Samuel L. Clemens __1__

3. Steamboats __6__

4. Halley's Comet __3__

5. *Tom Sawyer* __6__

Reading and Thinking

1. Mark Twain's real name was _____ Samuel Clemens

2. How many feet equal two fathoms?

   twelve

3. The main idea of paragraph 6 is
   ____ looking for gold.
   __✓__ Mark Twain's various jobs.
   ____ Halley's Comet.

Write the word that best completes each sentence.

4. I hope the raft doesn't _____ overturn _____ when we are on the lake.

   clutch   overturn   shiver

5. A person needs good _____ communication _____ skills to be an actor.

   communication   feature   comet

Working with Words

The prefix **im-** sometimes means "not." Add **im-** to each word. Then write its new meaning.

1. polite _____ impolite

   not polite

2. perfect _____ imperfect

   not perfect

3. possible _____ impossible

   not possible

4. patient _____ impatient

   not patient

5. The prefix **il-** can also mean "not." Write a definition for the word *illegal*.

   not legal

69

Knowing the Words

Write the words from the story that have the meanings below.

1. relatives of long ago

   ancestors
   (Par. 1)

2. book or journal for personal writing

   diary
   (Par. 7)

3. people who are new to a country

   immigrants
   (Par. 9)

4. Write this address without abbreviations.

   Dr. Sarah Jenkins
   50 E. North Temple St.
   Salt Lake City, UT 84150

   Doctor Sarah Jenkins

   50 East North Temple Street

   Salt Lake City, Utah 84150

Working with Words

Rewrite each group of words below using possessive forms.

1. the diary that belongs to Kim

   Kim's diary

2. the book that Alex owns

   Alex's book

3. the office used by two dentists

   dentists' office

4. the windows of a truck

   truck's windows

5. the library used by the students

   students' library

Reading and Thinking

1. What are Tom and his classmates going to make? _____ a family tree

2. Who wrote the book called *Roots*?

   Alex Haley

3. The author wrote this story to
   __✓__ inform readers about studying family history.
   ____ discuss the book *Roots*.
   ____ invite people to Salt Lake City, Utah.

4. Why did Miss Todd look at old letters?

   _____

   (Answers will vary.)

5. Read paragraph 7 from the story. Summarize the important information of the paragraph in one sentence.

   Family members can provide valuable

   information about family history.

Learning to Study

Look at the timeline and answer the questions below.

1. How many years does the line between each pair of dates stand for? __20__

2. Between which two dates did the rebuilding of the Statue of Liberty take place? _____ 1970–1990

71

Knowing the Words

Write the words from the story that have the meanings below.

1. place to sell many different items

   bazaar
   (Par. 1)

2. winding shapes

   spirals
   (Par. 2)

3. soaking through

   penetrating
   (Par. 3)

4. uneven

   irregular
   (Par. 3)

5. Write **S** between each pair of words that are synonyms, words with similar meanings.

   best ____ worst
   now __S__ immediately
   simple __S__ easy
   irregular __S__ uneven

Learning to Study

Complete this outline.

I. Things to do before tie-dying
   A. Fill a pan with warm water
   B. Fill another pan with hot water
   C. Place pans on newspaper
   D. Pour some dye into hot water

II. Things to do during tie-dying
   A. Wet cloth and squeeze
   B. Bunch cloth with rubber band
   C. Put cloth in dye and stir
   D. Remove cloth and rinse

Reading and Thinking

1. Number the events to show the order in which they happened.
   __1__ Susan introduced Mrs. Ellis.
   __5__ Susan rinsed out her cloth.
   __2__ Each group filled pans with water.
   __3__ Susan put a rubber band around the cloth.
   __4__ Susan put the cloth into the dye.

2. Why did Mrs. Ellis warn Susan not to put her hands in the dye?

   The dye would stain her hands.

   (Answers may vary.)

3. Read paragraph 2 from the story. Summarize the important information of the paragraph in one sentence.

   Tie-dying is a simple way to

   decorate cloth.
   (Answers may vary.)

4. Each group of students placed the pans of water on newspaper because _____

   they wanted to protect the tables

Working with Words

The prefix **mis-** means "badly" or "the opposite of." For example, the word *mistreat* means "to treat badly." Add **mis-** to each word in parentheses to complete the sentence.

1. Juan _____ misread _____ the map that was upside down. (read)

2. The child was _____ misbehaving _____ in the store. (behaving)

3. Julie _____ misplaced _____ her new pair of shoes. (placed)

73

Page 75

Write the words from the story that have the meanings below.

1. it seems that

   __apparently__
   (Par. 5)

2. a curved spark of electricity

   __arc__
   (Par. 11)

3. very intelligent person

   __genius__
   (Par. 14)

4. permits given for inventions

   __patents__
   (Par. 14)

5. Check the sentence in which *carry* has the same meaning it does in paragraph 10.

   ___ Rosa can't carry a tune.

   _✓_ An actor's voice must carry to the last row of seats.

   ___ Please carry my coat to the bus.

Learning to Study

Libraries arrange biographies in alphabetical order. They use the last name of the person who is the subject of the book. Number these biographies to show their order on a library shelf.

1. _3_ *The Life of Thomas Jefferson*
2. _2_ *Thomas A. Edison, Inventor*
3. _1_ *Marie Curie, Scientist*
4. _4_ *Up in Space With Sally Ride*

5. Check the subjects you could look up to learn more about Thomas Edison.

   _✓_ electric lights ___ mountains
   _✓_ phonographs ___ newspapers
   ___ flags _✓_ light bulb

Reading and Thinking

1. When did Edison invent his light bulb?

   __1879__

2. How old was Edison when he invented his vote recorder? __21__

3. Check the main idea of the story.
   ___ making long-distance calls
   _✓_ a famous inventor
   ___ the light bulb

4. Why was Edison called "The Wizard of Menlo Park"? _____

   __(Answers will vary.)__

5. The arc light couldn't be used indoors because __it was too bright__.

6. Why is Thomas Edison known as the greatest inventor in history?

   _____

   __(Answers will vary.)__

Working with Words

To make a plural word that does not end in s show ownership, add 's. For example, *the toys of the children* could be written *the children's toys*. Rewrite each group of words below. Use possessive forms.

1. sound of the geese __geese's sounds__
2. homes for the deer __deer's homes__
3. gloves of the women __women's gloves__
4. wool of the sheep __sheep's wool__
5. tails of the mice __mice's tails__

Page 77

Write the words from the story that have the meanings below.

1. very interesting

   __fascinating__
   (Par. 2)

2. convenient

   __handy__
   (Par. 2)

3. understandings between tribes

   __agreements__
   (Par. 2)

Circle the word with the correct meaning in each sentence below.

4. Anne decided to (write) right) a letter to her uncle.

5. Have you (scene, (seen)) my book about Sioux Indians?

Learning to Study

This is a map of some midwestern states. The map also shows the area where the Plains Indians lived. Look at the map and answer the questions below.

1. The Plains stretched from the Mississippi River on the east to the __Rocky Mountains__ on the west.

2. Is Nebraska north or south of Kansas?

   __north__

Reading and Thinking

1. Lance's ancestors were __Plains__ Indians.

2. What two areas were connected by a land bridge?

   __Siberia, present-day Alaska__

3. Why did the people cross the land bridge? __They were following the animals they needed for food.__
   (Answers may vary.)

4. Why did different tribes on the Plains use hand signals to communicate? __Because each tribe spoke a different language.__
   (Answers may vary.)

Write the word that best completes each sentence.

5. Lance __discovered__ many new facts about living in the wilderness.

   discovered traveled attached

6. High waves made the sea too __rough__ for sailing.

   lucky rough careful

7. What might have happened if the people hadn't crossed the land bridge into Alaska? _____
   __(Answers will vary.)__

Working with Words

After reading each sentence, write the compound word that correctly fills each blank.

1. Yoko found __seashells__ on the beach this morning. (seashells, rainbows)

2. I watched a lovely __sunset__ from my hotel room. (suntan, sunset)

Page 79

Write the words from the story that have the meanings below.

1. cloth

   __fabric__
   (Par. 1)

2. height

   __altitude__
   (Par. 7)

3. worth remembering

   __memorable__
   (Par. 7)

4. You have learned that idioms are groups of words that have special meanings. What does the idiom *in the clouds* mean?

   _____

   __(Answers will vary.)__

Working with Words

The suffix **-ous** usually means "full of" or "having." The suffix **-ous** can be added to nouns to change them to adjectives. Add the suffix **-ous** to these nouns. Then use each new word in a sentence.

1. thunder __thunderous__
   (Sentences will vary.)

2. humor __humorous__
   (Sentences will vary.)

Write the noun and suffix that form each adjective.

adjective	noun	suffix
3. courageous	courage	ous
4. poisonous	poison	ous

Reading and Thinking

1. Why did the first hot-air balloons just drift in the wind? __There was no way to control them.__ (Answers may vary.)

2. Why could Schantz re-light the burners after the balloon dropped to 18,000 feet? __There was more oxygen in the air.__

3. What hot-air ballooning records has Schantz set? __She set the women's record for staying in the air the longest and the world altitude record.__

4. Number the events to show the order in which they happened.

   _3_ Jetta Schantz set the hot-air balloon altitude record.

   _1_ The Montgolfier brothers demonstrated their balloon.

   _5_ Schantz set a record for staying up in the air in a balloon.

   _4_ Schantz received an award named after the Montgolfier brothers.

   _2_ Flight instruments began to be used in hot-air balloons.

Learning to Study

Complete this partial outline.

I. Important events in Jetta Schantz's life.

   A. __Set the hot-air balloon altitude record__

   B. __Received an international award named for the Montgolfier brothers__

   C. __Set a new women's record by staying in the air for 15 hours, 11 minutes__

Write a newspaper caption for the photo on page 78. _____

__(Answers will vary.)__

Page 81

Write the words from the story that have the meanings below.

1. usual kind

   __typical__
   (Par. 3)

2. a floor covering

   __ceramic tile__
   (Par. 3)

3. renewed or restored confidence

   __reassured__
   (Par. 6)

4. Write **S** between each pair of words that are synonyms, words with similar meanings.

helper	_S_	assistant
nervous	___	calm
doctor	_S_	physician
gently	___	roughly
remain	_S_	stay
healthy	_S_	well

Learning to Study

Complete this outline.

I. __Becoming a pet owner__

   A. Choosing the right pet

   B. Training your pet

II. __Caring for a pet__

   A. Getting your pet's shots

   B. Getting enough food and exercise

The yellow pages of the phone book provide helpful information when you need a phone number or an address. For example, if you needed a place for your pet to stay while you were on vacation, you could look in the yellow pages under the topic **kennels**. Suppose you needed a place to take your pet when it got sick. Under what topic could you look?

__veterinarians__

Reading and Thinking

Put **F** before each sentence that is a fact. Put **O** before each sentence that is an opinion.

1. _O_ Cats make better pets than dogs.
2. _F_ Many pets provide companionship.
3. _F_ Some veterinarians board animals for pet owners who are on vacation.
4. _O_ All children want to own a dog.

5. Check the words below that describe Dr. Collins.

   _✓_ caring _✓_ devoted
   ___ shy ___ upset

6. The author wrote this story to
   ___ talk about pets.
   _✓_ tell what a veterinarian does.
   ___ tell you about Meg's class.

Working with Words

To make a plural word that ends in s show ownership, add just an apostrophe. Rewrite each group of words below. Add an apostrophe to the underlined word to show ownership. One is done for you.

the toys of the __babies__ __babies' toys__

1. the windows of the __stores__
   __stores' windows__

2. the pencils that the __students__ use
   __students' pencils__

Rewrite each group of words below. Use possessive forms.

3. the coats that the men have
   __men's coats__

4. the feathers of the bird
   __bird's feathers__

Knowing the Words

Write the words from the story that have the meanings below.

1. soaked

   drenched
   (Par. 1)

2. part of a camera

   lens
   (Par. 11)

3. throw back an image

   reflex
   (Par. 11)

4. a book to hold pictures

   album
   (Par. 11)

5. **Personification** is a figure of speech in which an author talks about an idea or object as if it had lifelike qualities. Find the example of personification in paragraph 8 from the story.

   the bright sun greeted the girls

Learning to Study

Read this dictionary entry. Answer the questions below.

al bum /al´ bəm/ n **1** book with blank pages for holding stamps, photographs, etc. **2** a single long-playing record

1. What syllable is stressed when *album* is pronounced? _the first_

2. Which definition gives the meaning of *album* as it is used in paragraph 11? _1_

3. What part of speech is *album*? _noun_

4. Write the word *album* in syllables.

   al bum

Reading and Thinking

1. Check the main idea of the story.

   _✓_ taking good photographs

   ___ collecting photos

   ___ getting soaked in the rain

2. During what season do you think the story takes place? _early spring_

3. Why were there so few people at the zoo on the day that Betsy went to take pictures? _The weather was too cold._

   (Answers may vary.)

4. What is one difference between a range-finder camera and an SLR camera?

   An SLR camera uses several different lenses. (Answers may vary.)

Working with Words

You remember that the prefix **re-** means "again" or "back." Write words that have the following meanings by adding the prefix **re-** to a base word. Then use the new word in a sentence.

1. fill again _refill_

   (Sentences will vary.)

2. turn back _return_

   (Sentences will vary.)

The suffix **-ship** usually mean "a state or condition of being." Write the meaning of each word.

3. leadership _state or condition of being a leader_

4. township _state or condition of being a town_

83

Knowing the Words

Write the words from the story that have the meanings below.

1. go along with

   accompany
   (Par. 5)

2. story told with photographs

   photo essay
   (Par. 5)

3. several in a row

   series
   (Par. 6)

Learning to Study

Look at this diagram of one kind of newspaper press and answer the questions below.

1. How many plate cylinders does the press have? _two_

2. After the paper is printed, it is then _folded, cut, and trimmed_ .

Complete the following partial outline.

I. Making a Photo Essay

   A. _Take photographs_

   B. _Arrange photos to tell a story_

Reading and Thinking

1. Why did Betsy send some of her photographs to the magazine?

   Betsy wanted the magazine's editor to see what kind of work she could do.
   (Answers may vary.)

2. Betsy isn't beginning her summer job until June fifteenth because _she won't be finished with school until then_

3. What part of his summer job do you think Tom will enjoy the most? Why?

   (Answers will vary.)

4. Write one of the differences between a reporter and a photojournalist.

   (Answers will vary.)

5. Write one sentence the author used to show how Betsy felt at the beginning of the story. _"I got the job!" shrieked Betsy excitedly into the phone._
   (Answers may vary.)

Working with Words

The prefix **sub-** can mean "under" or "below." For example, the word *subway* means a train that travels under the ground. Add **sub-** to each word. Then write its new meaning.

1. marine _submarine_

   boat that travels underwater

2. normal _subnormal_

   below normal

8

Checking Understanding

Test 1   These exercises are to be completed after reading the story on page 10.

1. Number the events in the order in which they happened in the story.

   _3_ Ms. Lopez praises Tom's work.

   _2_ Tom meets with Ms. Lopez.

   _4_ Lance discusses the Festival.

   _5_ Betsy gets her assignment.

   _1_ Tom and Betsy wait to discuss their next assignments.

2. Tom is to focus on the ___ who benefit from the Festival.

   ___ organizers   _✓_ people

   ___ factories

3. Why did Lance call the Festival's organizers "the heart of our community"? _____

   (Answers will vary.)

4. Check two sentences that are true. (2)

   _✓_ The name of the school paper is *The Knightly News.*

   ___ Betsy is a reporter for the paper.

   _✓_ Unemployment is running high.

5. Check the main idea of the story.

   ___ taking good photographs

   _✓_ covering the Fall Festival

   ___ Tom's writing talent

6. Why was Tom surprised when Ms. Lopez praised his work? _____

   (Answers will vary.)

7. Many people in Kendall are without work because _the factory closed_ .

   Number of Words Read per Minute [ ]

Test 2   These exercises are to be completed after reading the story on page 22.

1. The Sierra Nevada lies ___ of San Francisco.

   _✓_ east   ___ south   ___ north

2. Check the sentences that are true. (2)

   _✓_ Ms. Lopez went mountain climbing at Yosemite National Park.

   _✓_ Kim took photos of the scenery.

   ___ The mountain air was warm.

   ___ Ann got lost in the mountains.

3. Why were the tracks of the climbers' snowshoes the only marks in the snow?

   (Answers will vary.)

4. Check the main idea of the story.

   ___ camping in the mountains

   _✓_ writing about mountain climbing

   ___ the importance of good snowshoes

5. Mountain climbers wear snowshoes to _make climbing easier_

6. It was a challenge to climb the mountain because _it was very high_

7. Why might the mountain's snowy ground be dangerous? _The ground may be slippery._

   Test Score (Possible Score — 8) [ ]

Checking Understanding

Test 3   These exercises are to be completed after reading the story on page 42.

1. Number the events in the order in which they happened in the story.

   _1_ The class met at *The Kendall Bulletin.*

   _2_ Mr. Martinez led the students to the newsroom.

   _3_ The students watched the typesetting machine.

   _5_ The students visited the press room.

   _4_ Layout sheets were fed into the camera.

2. Write the names of two *Bulletin* departments the students visited. (2) (Accept any two of these answers.)

   newsroom, composing room, press room

3. Why does the make-up crew place each story on a layout sheet? _to see how each page of the paper will look_

4. Check two sentences that are true. (2)

   ___ The *Bulletin* camera is small.

   _✓_ The make-up crew places each story on a layout sheet.

   _✓_ The *Bulletin* is folded and cut.

5. Check the main idea of the story.

   ___ interviewing a reporter

   ___ taking a class trip

   _✓_ watching the newspaper process

6. Why do you think Tom's class visited the *Bulletin*? _They wanted to see the newspaper process._

   Number of Words Read per Minute [ ]

   Test Score (Possible Score — 8) [ ]

Test 4   These exercises are to be completed after reading the story on page 62.

1. The study of stars is called ___.

   ___ geology   _✓_ astronomy

   ___ galaxy

2. Check two sentences that are true. (2)

   _✓_ The stars move.

   _✓_ The sun is a star.

   ___ Stars never explode.

3. Write two reasons the *Bulletin* prints a night-sky map. (2)

   to show what stars are visible and to show the stars' positions

4. Check the main idea of this story.

   ___ astronomy books

   ___ space travel in future years

   _✓_ interesting facts about stars

5. Astronomers use large telescopes to ___.

   ___ see the brightest stars

   _✓_ study the most distant stars

6. Why don't astronomers know exactly how many stars exist? _There are too many stars to count._

   Test Score (Possible Score — 8) [ ]

86